Interior Decorat

Created and Designed by the Editorial Staff of Ortho Books

Project Editor
Jane Horn

Writer
Christina Nelson

Illustrator
Mitzi McCarthy

Principal Photographer
David Livingston

Ortho Books

Publisher
Richard E. Pile, Jr.

Editorial Director
Christine Jordan

Production Director
Ernie S. Tasaki

Managing Editors
Robert J. Beckstrom
Michael D. Smith
Sally W. Smith

System Manager
Linda M. Bouchard

Marketing Specialist
Daniel Stage

Sales Manager
Thomas J. Leahy

Distribution Specialist
Barbara F. Steadham

Technical Consultant
J. A. Crozier, Jr., Ph.D.

Editorial Coordinator
Cass Dempsey

Copyeditor
Barbara Feller-Roth

Proofreader
Deborah Bruner

Indexer
Trisha Feuerstein

Editorial Assistant
John Parr

Composition by
Laurie A. Steele

Production by
Studio 165

Separations by
Color Tech Corp.

Lithographed in the USA by
Webcrafters, Inc.

Special Thanks to
Agnes Bourne
Boussac
Decorator's Walk
Jack Lenor Larsen
The San Francisco Decorator
 Showcase 1991
Slips

Address all inquiries to:
Ortho Books
Box 5047
San Ramon, CA 94583-0947

Copyright © 1992
Monsanto Company
All rights reserved under international and Pan-American copyright conventions.

  3 4 5 6 7 8 9
  94 95 96 97 98

ISBN 0-89721-245-2
Library of Congress Catalog Card
Number 92-70586

THE SOLARIS GROUP

6001 Bollinger Canyon Road
San Ramon, CA 94583

Designers
Names of designers are followed by the page numbers on which their work appears.
R = right, C = center,
L = left, T = top, B = bottom.
Richard M. Banks; San Francisco: 107R
Nancy Bernard, Nancy Bernard Interiors, Walnut Creek, Calif.: 101
Claudia Bordin; San Bruno, Calif.: 107L
Agnes Bourne, A.S.I.D.; San Francisco: 104
Diane Chapman; San Francisco: front cover TL, CL, B; 64; 65; 88; 94; 96; 106; back cover TR
Childs-Dreyfus Group; Chicago: 97
Jan Cox; Sun Valley, Idaho: 97
Davidon Homes: 52
Melinda Douglas; Los Angeles: 71
R. Germain Fontana, San Francisco: 61
Allison Holland; Honolulu, Hawaii: 102
Barbara Jacobs; Saratoga, Calif.: 58
Sharon D. Kasser; Menlo Park, Calif.: 100
Karen Kitowski; San Francisco: 25
Andrew Lau, Andrew Lau Interior Design, San Francisco: 26
Linda and Steven Marks, Inside OUT Design; San Francisco: 66
Charlene Martoza and Tina Martinez, Furniture Art Studio: 9
James Miller, AIA, and Associates: 67
Miller/Stein; Palo Alto, Calif.: 4–5
Jan Moyer Design, lighting designer; Berkeley, Calif.: 84
Lyn Peterson, Motif Design; New Rochelle, N.Y.: 50–51
Pizazz Interior Design, Lafayette, Calif.: 10
Esther Reilly; Palo Alto, Calif.: 13
Lindy Smallwood; Danville, Calif.: front cover CR; 7
William Ellis Smith; Hollywood, Calif.: 12
Gayle Walter; Pebble Beach, Calif.: 11
Kitty Woodworth Interiors; Lafayette, Calif.: 39, 78, 80

Photographers
Names of photographers are followed by the page numbers on which their work appears. All other photography is by David Livingston.
R = right, C = center,
L = left, T = top, B = bottom.

Russell Abraham: 11, 13, 58
Hedrich Blessing: 97T
Michael Garland: 12 (reprinted from *Home Magazine*, copyright 1991, Hachette Publications, Inc.)
Kari Haavisto: 50–51 (reprinted from *Home Magazine*, copyright 1991, Hachette Publications, Inc.), 108R
Michael Jensen: 92–93, 97B
Jenifer Jordon: 109
Stephen Marley: 105
Keith Scott Morton: 36–37, 94, 98, 99, 101T, 108L
Kenneth Rice: 9, 10, 26, 52, 61, 66, 67, 84, 101, 104, 107L
Jeffrey Westman: title page, 3T, 39, 65R, 78, 80, 91

Front Cover
Good taste and style can be expressed in many ways, as the diversity of these beautifully designed rooms demonstrates.

Title Page
Garden tones of soothing, peaceful greens, enlivened with a touch of rose, create a calm and serene mood in a sophisticated family room.

Page 3
Top: A surprisingly spacious eating area was carved out of a tight corner by using a combination of seating: banquette on two sides of the table and pull-up chairs on the other two sides.

Bottom: Children respond to color in their personal living spaces.

Back Cover
Top left: Sky blues and dreamy whites always pair well.
Top right: Groups of pictures look best when framed alike.
Bottom left: The soft blue-green walls of this old-fashioned bathroom have a mottled, cloudlike look.
Bottom right: The mood is Southwest and country in this uncluttered, very appealing master bedroom.

Interior Decorating

KEYS TO CREATING A PERSONAL STYLE

Decorating your home to enhance its appearance, improve its function, and reflect your personal tastes can be immensely satisfying, whether you're redoing your home completely or simply sprucing up spaces here and there. But creating a personal decorating style and developing it into a workable design doesn't happen overnight. It's an evolutionary process that centers as much on knowing yourself and your family living patterns as it does on decorating basics. One key to unlocking your own style is recognizing how to match personal tastes— what you like visually and aesthetically—with what will really serve the space and the people who use it on a daily basis. Another key to achieving results that will please you now, and later, is to plan carefully so that you know exactly what suits you and the space before you buy. This book is intended to help you build confidence in making decorating decisions by supplying the information and tools you'll need to translate ideas into solutions. It is organized as a workbook to guide you through the various steps that go into developing a design. The first chapter focuses on providing the framework on which to create a personal decorating style, whether you choose to be your own interior designer or seek the assistance of a professional.

A well-designed room is more than just a pretty space. It also satisfies the personal needs of the people who use it every day.

DEFINING YOUR PERSONAL STYLE

Creating a personal decorating style requires more than knowing your preferences in, let's say, color combinations or furnishings. It also involves examining such key issues as function, livability, comfort, family composition, and budget. It has to do with defining the look and mood you wish for your rooms, with the overall feeling you wish for your home.

How Your Home Feels

Describing the overall feeling you wish your home to have can be a valuable first step in deciding how you want its rooms to look and function. Do you wish your home to be a haven from the busy, sometimes hectic, world? Your bedroom a retreat from the children and the work place? Do you wish your home to be a gathering place for family and friends? The kitchen a lively center of communal activity? If you live in a northern climate where the winters are long and cold, do you want to feel snug and secure? Or, wherever you reside, do you prefer an airy

indoor-outdoor atmosphere within your living spaces? Do you wish the mood of your home to be mostly fun or serious, modest or grand, earthy or eccentric? Coming up with a concept for your home as a whole, and keeping it in mind throughout the design process,

can help the various rooms work together smoothly on both a practical and an aesthetic level.

What is the Tone?

One way to determine how you want your home to appear and function is to consider the general decorating look you prefer. Is it formal, where furniture arrangements tend to be symmetrical, the mood adult-like and reserved, and the overall effect dressy? Or is it somewhat informal, where furnishings are designed to be used and grouped in a casual manner and the atmosphere caters to all ages? Perhaps you're most at home with a semiformal

look, where formal and informal elements share space, and furnishings may be either dressed up or down according to the occasion.

Formal

Picturing a formal room often evokes images of traditional settings, but contemporary interiors can be formal as well. Formal rooms are often associated with expensive materials and smooth textures: polished hardwoods, chrome, marble, glass; fabrics such as silk and velvet; perhaps crystal and silver accessories. From a maintenance standpoint, formal rooms demand lots of upkeep—those smooth, shiny

Polished woods, luxurious fabrics, and traditional furniture arrangements create a formal look.

surfaces show every stain and speck of dust. If you're drawn to a formal look, you probably enjoy neat, well-ordered rooms. Just bear in mind that active youngsters and indoor pets normally don't mix with formal arrangements.

Informal

In an active family informal interiors usually wear relatively well, largely because furnishings and materials are casual in style, rough textured, and generally durable: woods such as unpolished pine, oak, and ash; fabrics with nubby or uneven surfaces; perhaps pottery or copper accessories rather than porcelain or brass. A fireplace in an informal room might have a brick or slate surround rather than marble.

One advantage of informal rooms is that their rougher, duller surfaces—although not necessarily easier to clean than polished surfaces—show dirt less readily. Informal rooms have a more relaxing air, partly because the furnishings are less stiff and upright than their formal counterparts, and their arrangements usually less symmetrical. Many of the so-called country decorating styles can be described as informal.

Semiformal

Not surprisingly, semiformal rooms fall somewhere between formal and informal and may be designed to lean more heavily one way or the other. For example, a roomful of informal furnishings may be arranged in a symmetrical manner about a formal focal-point fireplace. Or the cool, crisp formality of a sleek, modern kitchen may be softened with warm, informal accessories.

One advantage of well-planned semiformal settings is their versatility. Semiformal can be a good solution when you'd like the wardrobe of your room to be sometimes dressy, sometimes not, as when a family-oriented living room is pressed into service for formal entertaining, or a home office is spiffed up for weekend guests. You can alter the personality of a semiformal room with some quick-change artistry: pull off the childproof slipcovers to reveal a beautifully upholstered sofa (or, conversely, put on identical slipcovers to unify the appearance of mismatched chairs); replace cotton toss pillows with silk, wood candlesticks with silver, an informal bowl of daisies with a gracious vase of roses. If you're thinking of decorating your home in an eclectic manner, you may find yourself attracted to a semiformal look.

Informal settings are low-key and relaxed. Upkeep is manageable because casual furnishings and fabrics tend to be relatively durable.

Although the furnishings are contemporary, their symmetrical arrangement gives this living room a semiformal air.

DECORATING STYLES

The right style—your style—is yours for the making. It might be a variation of a style with certain historical or cultural connections, one with a regional emphasis, or a traditional favorite born from your own family roots.

Choosing Your Style

Usually, it's not too difficult to determine whether your tastes tend toward formal or informal. It's not as easy to pinpoint a decorating style. A glance at titles in a bookstore or library reveals so many individually named styles that the prospect of finding the one that's right for you and the space you are decorating may seem intimidating. You may discover that you're not attracted to a specific style but rather to a variation. Your style might develop around a theme or out of respect for the architectural character of your home. It might even evolve from pictures and places you've seen.

How to Decide

A good way to begin developing your own style is to examine decorating styles in a broad way. Do you prefer traditionally styled houses, or do you find yourself partial to contemporary settings? Do you prefer rooms filled with collections and organized clutter or those that are mainly functional? Do the light woods and homespun effects of country styles attract your attention? What about interiors that cleverly intermix the old and new—modern sofas with antique side chairs, for example?

Think about the homes you've seen whose decorating style appeals to you. What is it that you like in particular? Would the features that attract your attention mesh with your own living patterns? The family's? Walk by room settings in furniture and department stores; visit model homes and designer show houses; leaf through books and magazines. Although the materials and furnishings of designer show houses are usually beyond the range of most pocketbooks, they can be excellent sources of inspiration and decorating ideas. Pay attention to what you like: What looks, moods, and styles express something of the personal style you are seeking to create? Will they be comfortable and functional in your home? What *won't* work in your own environment?

As you consider decorating styles, it might be helpful to refer to the following descriptions of four broad categories of styles: country, traditional, modern, and eclectic. They will familiarize you with just some of the looks, materials, and moods associated with each category. You'll discover that many individual styles cross boundaries and may fall easily into one category or another. The Shaker style, for example, might be viewed as a regional country style because of its basic simplicity of appearance and materials; but Shaker also

has strong traditional ties—its roots belong to a specific period in American history. Furthermore, the term *Shaker* is often applied to a furniture style much admired for its fine workmanship and simple lines.

Start a File

As you review the possibilities among styles, begin gathering ideas and collecting pictures and information to set up a series of files to help you decide what you really like—and dislike. One of the files can be dedicated entirely to styles. Others might be devoted to objects such as furnishings, lamps, accessories; materials; colors; and "inspirations" on how you want your home to feel. Later, when you're planning actual spaces, developing color schemes, and deciding on finishes, you can expand these files to include more specific information—from paint chips and fabric swatches to lists of resources. You'll find the files invaluable in helping focus on what you might like to add to your home—and in seeing what you already have that can be used in new and imaginative ways.

Traditional Style

Those who favor the historic look and wish to maintain a connection with the past find traditional styles appealing. Sometimes the reference is to a particular period in time—Georgian, for instance—or to a particular style of furnishings, such as Queen Anne or Art Nouveau. Often, though, decorating in the traditional style simply means recreating an

image of the past by adapting traditional motifs, classic furnishings, and time-honored materials to present-day rooms and life-styles. One reason that traditional remains a recurring favorite is that its materials are tried and true, its ambience perceived as timeless.

A good deal of formality, elegance, ornament, and luster (not to mention high maintenance) is associated with most traditional interiors: fine hardwoods, polished to perfection; upholstery rather than slipcovers; windows layered with fabric; gleaming lamps and hardware. Some traditional looks, however, are less formal, especially if they have country roots. A home decorated in a New England Colonial style, for instance, might be dubbed rustic traditional or refined country.

Traditional decorating styles in American homes reach back to the 1700s for their gracious, sometimes aristocratic looks and carry into the early decades of this century. They may be grouped roughly into two categories, classical and period, within which many individual styles can be found.

Classical Styles

The classical styles turn to ancient Greece and Rome for inspiration and incorporate design principles from art and architecture, paying particular attention to such matters as formal symmetry, balance, scale, and proportion. American Federal and French Empire are examples of this style, in which furnishings, patterns in wallcoverings and fabrics, even finishing touches such as mirror frames carry distinctly classical themes. Some typical motifs are acanthus leaves, vase and urn shapes, delicately detailed columns, and elaborately carved moldings.

Period Styles

As the name suggests, period styles owe their appearance to a specific period in history that left its mark on the culture and peoples of the time. Period styles are many and varied, recalling primarily English and French monarchies and early American interiors, of both the wealthy and the humble. Typically, the furnishings of the period influence the decoration of the room; in some cases, the style derives its name from that of the cabinetmaker rather than royalty. (You can read more about specific furniture styles in the chapter titled "Developing Your Design," beginning on page 51.) Among the more familiar traditional period styles from the eighteenth century are the English-American Queen Anne and Georgian; the French Louis XV, sometimes referred to as Rococo; and the French Louis XVI. Some early-nineteenth-century period styles include the German-influenced Biedermeier and Shaker, both embraced by the common man. Federal and Empire, mentioned above, may be thought of as both period and classical styles. Later in the 1800s decorating styles with architectural connections (such as Gothic Revival and High Renaissance) filled Victorian interiors; but by the end of the

era, a less stuffy and less historical view of traditional was coming into focus and setting the tone for traditional styles as interpreted today.

Throughout both centuries, oriental furnishings and accessories, with their lacquered finishes and traditional motifs, contributed to both classical and period rooms. In some instances East joined West to produce such classic furniture styles as Chinese Chippendale and Arts and Crafts.

Traditional Materials and Moods

• Materials in the traditional style include furnishings constructed of fine hardwoods, such as mahogany, rosewood, walnut, and cherry; lacquered and veneered surfaces; reproduction pieces; finely crafted antiques.
• Floors of stained and polished hardwoods or marble; thick-pile carpets, oriental rugs.
• Fabrics such as silk, damask, velvet; intricate patterns, large

florals, historic designs, and crewelwork; windows treated with draperies, valances, swags, and fabric-covered cornices.
• Accessories of brass, porcelain, crystal, and silver; fringes, tassels; emphasis on details, such as moldings, hardware, and picture and mirror frames.
• The following describe traditional style: elegant, gracious, formal, timeless, classic, artfully cluttered, old world, patrician, handsome, finely detailed, elaborate, rich.

The traditional elements of this elegant French bedroom are unmistakable: period furnishings, draped fabrics, decorative wood paneling, and marble floors.

Country Style

There are so many different interpretations of country style that adopting, or adapting, a country theme presents almost infinite possibilities. On the same suburban street, you can have the feeling of a rustic New England farmhouse or a charming English cottage; in almost any neighborhood the aura of the French countryside; in a big-city loft the simplicity associated with rural living. American country styles in particular seem to have captured interest around the time of the United States bicentennial, in the mid to late 1970s, and have, if anything, gained even more popularity in recent years.

American Country

A sampler of American country styles might include a number with strong historical ties—Early Colonial, Shaker, and Pennsylvania Dutch, for example—most of them characterized by simplicity of furnishings and materials and a traditional, even primitive, mood. Then there are the regional country styles that may be traditional or not—Adirondack, for instance, or Southwest. Another category, coined simply American country, has become a style unto itself; noted for its warm, comfortable mood, American country often includes classic country elements from different regions and different periods of history.

European Country

Just about every European nation offers a country style. Country in the Mediterranean has an indoor-outdoor feeling, with an accent on simple, practical furnishings. In the more northerly climates, natural textures and fabrics prevail, and decorative detailing on furniture, walls, and floors is common. English country is known for its cozy, cluttered look and floral patterns; the French focus is on countrified versions of courtly furnishings from different periods in history.

Dressed-Up Country

Although most country interiors are informal in their appearance and mood, it is possible to achieve a stylish, semiformal look by dressing up fabrics, window coverings, and accessories for a refined, rustic mix—the country manor, if you will, instead of the country cottage. An even more formal atmosphere can be attained by combining elegant traditional furnishings with simple country pieces, for example, or by juxtaposing highly polished woods with textured floor and wall surfaces, or by mixing folk art with fine art. The effect can suggest a town-and-country, rather than a town or country, setting.

Country Materials and Moods

• Among the materials and moods common to a number of country styles are furnishings generally of light woods, such as pine, oak, maple, and ash—often with bleached, distressed, painted, or natural finishes—but also of darker hardwoods, such as walnut and pecan; also wicker, rattan, bamboo, cane, and willow; handcrafted furnishings and unrestored antiques.

• Floors of stone, brick, and quarry tile; plain floorboards left bare, painted, or covered with scatter rugs or floor cloths.

• Fabrics such as cotton (corduroy, chintz, and ticking), linen, and wool; gingham, plaid, small florals, and paisleys; simple window treatments, plain curtains, and shutters.

• Accessories identified with the country life: baskets, folk art, quilts, boxes, and farm implements.

• The following describe country style: carefree, informal, comfortable, comforting, homespun, relaxed, folksy, easy care, warm, welcoming, simple, fresh, primitive, peasantlike, unpretentious, natural.

Country style is unpretentious and comfortable yet always fresh and inviting.

Modern Style

The modern movements in general share a common philosophy: a rejection of the historical connections, cluttered arrangements, and excessive ornamentation identified with so many traditional styles in favor of designs and furnishings that are clean lined, straightforward, functional, and never fussy.

Modern interiors tend to be fairly open in their floor plans and understated in their colors, patterns, and textures so as to draw attention to the architecture of the room and give an impression of spaciousness. They may be sleekly formal with gleaming materials of glass, steel, chrome, marble, and polished granite; or informally outfitted with glass block, tile, and laminate.

Some modern-style rooms take the minimalist approach—sparsely furnished but not necessarily uncomfortable—and may appear austere without being antiseptic. Others may have a look that's sometimes called softly modern, a description often interchanged with contemporary: light and airy in mood, comfortably furnished with pieces that are neither traditional in appearance nor harshly modern, easy to maintain, and eminently livable.

Art Deco

In this country, modern styles are thought to have begun in the late 1920s with Art Deco, a design movement that took its inspiration from a transcultural mixture of primitive art, classic architecture, and modern motifs, and repackaged them to reflect the clean, functional lines and industrial themes of the technological advances of

the times. The geometric forms, zigzag patterns, and curvilinear detailing of Art Deco designs continue to be integrated into present-day interiors, as applied decoration to walls, in lighting fixtures, or as accessories.

Bauhaus

The modern movement gained momentum in this country after World War II as an outgrowth of the European Bauhaus philosophy, which encouraged designers from all fields to use technology to create objects for everyday life that were both functional and beautiful. After experiencing some sterile moments, where the goals of comfort and livability were often stifled in the name of pure function, the movement eased into a few major styles that are prevalent today, such as high tech and postmodern.

High Tech

As its name implies, high-tech style derives much of its appearance and many of its materials from advances in electronics and space technology. Sophisticated computerized appliances, state-of-the-art audiovisual equipment, industrial-look lighting, laminate cabinetry with black-glass doors, and high-gloss surfaces are just a few of the elements common to high-tech rooms.

Postmodern

The postmodern style follows the modernist philosophy of simplicity and function, but it reinstates some of the traditional elements found in homes of the past—details such as moldings and ornamentation,

pattern, and texture. This connection doesn't attempt to imitate the past but alludes to it, often in a lighthearted, whimsical way.

Contemporary

Although the term *contemporary* is sometimes used in an offhand way to describe a room that's not traditional in appearance, contemporary is also considered a decorating style in and of itself. A contemporary home usually contains versatile furnishings that do not suggest a particular period but blend together in arrangements that fit the space visually and aesthetically. A contemporary room doesn't typically contain antiques or reproduction pieces, nor does it look especially modern; it adapts admirably to an informal life-style.

Modern Materials and Moods

• In a modern interior you might find materials of this type: furnishings of stainless steel, chrome, leather, canvas, glass, Plexiglas, molded plastics, and light-colored, highly polished woods; modular seating.

• Large expanses of glass with minimal window treatments, to permit maximum natural light.

• Fabrics of natural materials, such as woven cotton, grass cloth, and wool; wall-to-wall carpeting.

• Accessories are usually few, to maintain the uncluttered look, but might include abstract art, sculpture, and plants.

• The following describe the modern style: minimal, sparse, Spartan, bare, clean lined, simple, spacious, edited, disciplined, uncluttered, austere, industrial.

This airy dining room is clean-lined and spare, typical of modern interiors. Comfortable seating and a playful use of color are welcoming notes.

Eclectic Style

Decorating in the eclectic style brings a thoughtful mixture of furnishings, finishes, and accessories to a room or a collection of rooms. Of all the styles, eclectic is perhaps the most challenging to put together because in a sense there are no rules—no examples for reference, as you might have with a Georgian, French Provincial, or high-tech interior—and each room is uniquely its own. There are no typical materials, no special looks, no particular moods. Eclectic design is challenging, too, because it takes just the right combination of ingredients to ensure that each item retains its own flavor while contributing to the unity of the room as a whole.

Personal Expression

Decorating in an eclectic manner can be highly rewarding because the results are a true expression of personal style. You might begin with a period theme, for instance, and personalize it with possessions that reflect your own experiences. You might combine traditional furnishings from several eras in a contemporary setting. Or build a room around a single focal point—a finely detailed fireplace or a medieval tapestry—or a collection of some type. You might seek a rather formal, cosmopolitan look by pulling together fine examples of furniture from several different countries, or aim for friendly informality by introducing ethnic fabrics and accessories into an otherwise American setting. You might even begin with an empty room and go from there, following your own instincts.

Be Confident

As an expression of personal style, the eclectic approach usually works most successfully when you have confidence in your own tastes, imagination, and the time and patience for extra planning—time to think about how to unify the individual elements to tie the room together, time to consider the sizes and proportions of different styles of furniture and to experiment with various arrangements until you achieve the results that satisfy you most. Taking an eclectic route is sometimes more costly than a more conventional one, largely because it is the quality of each item selected as well as the quality of the design that make the space work.

The success of eclectic design—regardless of whether you mix periods or nationalities; prefer traditional, country, or modern styles; or spend moderately or lavishly—depends on combining individuality with physical comfort, function, and livability.

An eclectic interior, such as this cottage living room, is an expression of personal style.

KNOWING YOUR LIFE-STYLE

It makes more sense to enter a decorating project with a clear picture of how you and your family live than to have to adjust or modify your plans later on.

How You Really Live

Creating the look and selecting the style that suits you best involves knowing your own life-style intimately and assessing it honestly. A pair of pure white chintz loveseats in the living room may fit your envisioned neutral color scheme, but they're not practical if you have small children and pets. Of course, you could keep family activities off-limits, but a more practical and understanding solution might be to invest in a family-friendly fabric that's durable, doesn't show soil, and still works in a neutral color scheme.

What Are Your Needs?

One advantage to assessing your life-style is that it helps you become more aware of what you and your room need from your decorating project. If you examine why you're planning to redecorate, you may discover that some of your needs may be psychological. Perhaps you feel that the room needs more privacy, or a more intimate mood, or a more cheerful atmosphere. Perhaps your need to make some changes comes from dissatisfaction with the way things look—the television in plain sight, the dated wallcovering in the front entry, the worn carpet on the stairs. You and your family may also have clear physical needs that are fueling your project: the decision to set up a home office, for instance; the need for another bedroom as the family grows; the demand for more storage in the living areas.

Although the subject of meeting psychological and physical needs is addressed more fully in the chapter titled "Planning Your Spaces" (page 33), it might be helpful for you to make a list of those needs as you see them in these early planning stages. You can add to the list as you become more involved in your project.

The life-style survey on the next two pages may be useful in guiding you through some of the preliminary decision-making essential to your decorating plan.

All the comforts beckon in this thoughtfully planned study. There is an area for lounging, a spot to stretch out and read, and a place to work on the day's mail.

Surveying Your Life-Style: Know Thyself

Recognizing your tastes, examining the makeup of your family, and seeing how you and those around you really live are key to the success of your decorating project. The following questions will help you evaluate your life-style; the checklist at the end of each section is intended to assist you in keeping track of your answers. Be sure to have all family members take part in the exercise.

Family Composition

How many family members are living at home? Number of adults? Children and their ages? Do you expect the numbers to change over the next few years? Are you planning to expand your family? Will some children be leaving home for college or jobs? Do your parents or other relatives reside with you or visit frequently? Are they elderly or disabled or do they have other special needs? If grandchildren visit, what are their needs? How about pets? Do they live indoors or out, or come and go at will? If they're mainly inside pets, what are their demands and requirements?

☐ Primary family and ages
☐ Other family members and ages
☐ Special needs of users
☐ Frequent visitors (family or not)
☐ Pets and their needs

Your Home and Its Spaces

Do you live in the city, the suburbs, or a rural environment? In an apartment, a house, a condominium? An old or a new building? Does climate, location, or the age of your home influence how you live and use its spaces? What about its exposure to sun and shade, noise, traffic, and neighbors? Will these factors influence your decorating plans? How long do you intend to live here? One year, five years, indefinitely? Does your home have enough space to grow with your family? Are you planning to decorate for your own pleasure, appearance' sake, improved function, or resale value? Are there any special structural problems that need correction before you can implement a decorating plan, or are the problems mainly cosmetic?

Make a list of your dissatisfactions, from the most problematic to the least: poor layout, not enough privacy, inadequate storage, too little light, worn carpets, faded upholstery, tired color scheme. Make another list of what you like about your home and would probably not change.

Now, ask the same questions of the room (or rooms) you're thinking of redoing first, noting the good points and what needs improvement. Again make a list of likes and dislikes about the space. For instance, a particular room may get a lot of traffic noise, or feel dark and cold because of its northerly location, or simply not function well because of its furniture arrangement.

☐ Location of home and its influence on life-style
☐ Impact of climate or seasonal changes
☐ Orientation to view, neighbors, street, sun, shade, wind
☐ Length of occupancy
☐ Good points
☐ Problems and/or dissatisfactions
☐ Which room first and why
☐ Lists of decorating priorities for home and room

Family Activities

How does your family spend time together at home? Dining, reading, conversing, listening to music, watching TV and videos, playing board games? What about hobbies and sports? Where do you eat family meals? Participate in other activities? How do you feel about electronic equipment (especially the TV) being in plain sight? Would you conceal it if you could? Is family togetherness usually a happy event? Stressful? Boring? Is there enough space and privacy for individual members to carry out their own special interests without hindrance? Are there any hobbies, personal talents, athletic or artistic accomplishments to take into account in your decorating plans? Collections, mementos, photographs, artwork, trophies that are connected with family or individual activities?

☐ Shared family activities pursued at home
☐ Individual activities pursued at home
☐ Special considerations for special interests
☐ Which rooms are devoted to which activities?
☐ How you feel about the placement of the TV
☐ Spatial needs for various activities
☐ Storage needs for equipment, games, toys, et cetera

Entertaining Style

How do you prefer to entertain? Formally, casually, semiformally? Infrequently or all the time? In the dining room, living room, kitchen, outdoors? Large groups or small? Sit-down dinners or stand-up buffets? Do you serve foods on fine china, informal ware, or paper plates? Do you handle the cooking when you entertain, use a caterer, encourage potlucks, take your guests out to a restaurant? Do your children entertain their friends at home? How often? Birthdays, sleepovers, teen parties?

☐ Formal entertaining needs
☐ Casual entertaining needs
☐ Adequate space to seat and serve guests
☐ Adequate storage for linens, table settings, and so on
☐ Children's special entertaining needs
☐ Special-occasion needs

Housekeeping Concerns

How would you describe yourself as a housekeeper? Compulsively neat? Moderately tidy? Disorganized? Resigned? What are the habits of other family members? Do you tackle housecleaning on your own, enlist others, use hired help? Do you like everything hidden behind closed doors? Displayed on open shelves? Are easy-to-maintain materials important to you? What about laundry—does your family have lots or little? Who shares in that chore? Do you send clothing out to be laundered, or do you wash and iron the items yourself? Is the laundry area set up with enough storage, hanging, and work space?

How do you handle household disposables? Where do you store cans, glass, plastics, paper, and other materials to be recycled? Do you need special areas for this purpose? In the garage? In the kitchen? How about potentially hazardous wastes, such as cleaning products, paint thinner, pesticides?

☐ General upkeep and chores
☐ Laundry space and storage
☐ Division of labor for housekeeping duties
☐ Storing household staples and supplies
☐ Recycling program

Working at Home

What kind of a home office do you require? Do you simply need a place to pay bills, plan meals, and write letters, or do you need a center to accommodate both home- and office-related work? Do your interests demand lots of horizontal work space, or will a tall, narrow area do just as well? If you do professional work at home on a regular basis, do you have enough space to dedicate a specific area to desk work, computers, fax and copy machines, and storage? Where can that space come from? If you bring professional work home on occasion, or require a personal home office, can you convert a portion of an existing room to satisfy your needs? What about a little-used closet, a part of a hall, or a balcony? Have you considered multipurpose furnishings that lend themselves to office and home use? Do your children need officelike space to do their homework (with computer, typewriter, shelves, and so on)?

☐ Personal home office needs
☐ Professional home office requirements
☐ Finding space for an office
☐ Making room for the computer and related equipment
☐ Adequate lighting and electrical outlets
☐ Multiuse rooms with some office space
☐ Multiuse furnishings

Storage Considerations

What are your views on storage? Do you like to keep your rooms free of clutter and everything but the essentials tucked away? Do you prefer hall closets to coatracks? Books and magazines shelved rather than displayed? Children's toys in bins, not on the floor?

A favorite room is not just the one that looks the best, but is also the one that you feel most comfortable being in. Part of the decorating process is to determine how that space would best serve your needs.

Where do you store large, bulky items—basement, attic, or garage? What about out-of-season clothing, luggage, Christmas decorations, gardening supplies? What do you do with hard-to-handle items such as the table tennis platform, bicycles, sports and fitness equipment? Where do you store valuable documents? Some documents, such as investment portfolios and insurance policies, need to be kept current and therefore readily accessible; others, such as old tax returns, can be stored but should be relatively easy to retrieve if necessary. Where do you keep your documents—in boxes in the attic or basement? In a file cabinet, desk drawer, back corner of the closet? Could you find them in a pinch?

☐ Open shelving and its place in your home
☐ Closed storage
☐ Storage potential within living spaces
☐ Storing oversize, hard-to-hide items
☐ Storing outdoor equipment
☐ Storing athletic equipment
☐ Storing documents

CONSIDERING THE REALITIES

Now that you have a sense of the decorative style you prefer and what you hope to accomplish, it's essential to consider some down-to-earth issues: your budget; the structural limitations of your house or room; and your own limitations in terms of time, skills, and energy.

Financial Limitations

Budget is a key issue in almost any home-improvement project. For the fortunate few with unlimited dollars to pour into the interior design of their home, budget is less of a concern; even structural and personal limitations become less important because the budget can be adjusted to pay for professional assistance or cover any remodeling costs that might precede a decorating plan. Since most homeowners don't enjoy a bottomless pocketbook, however, figuring out how much money it will take—and how best to allocate it—become critical issues. And though no one likes to watch every penny, constraints can be beneficial because they encourage careful planning.

As you prepare a budget, consider the various facets of your decorating plans. Will this be a short-term project involving just one or perhaps two rooms? If you eventually intend to redo the entire house, will it add value to the property? If you expect to live in this home for just a few years, is it worth investing large

quantities of time and money? Or are you redecorating solely to prepare the house for resale? If so, will you regain the money spent in the selling price? Even homeowners with the most carefully planned budgets discover that costs usually run higher than anticipated. Do you have the resources, or a contingency plan, should your costs exceed your budget?

The specifics of the budget you prepare at this early stage of the project will likely change as your design takes shape, but your goal should be to keep the final figure as close to this preliminary one as possible. For example, you may discover that the flooring material you eventually select costs more than you had allocated, so you may have to trim costs elsewhere. The more information you can gather now, the better picture you will have of the entire project from a financial point of view.

Remember, too, that your budget will be a constant factor throughout the decorating process. Keeping within its limits will help you stay in control of your project and achieve a successful outcome. In fact, the constraints of the budget may encourage you to find creative but less expensive alternatives

that can help keep costs in line yet still allow you to get the results you want.

Personal Limitations

Budgeting time and energy and recognizing your skills and limitations are other issues to consider. Even what seems a simple decorating job can be disruptive to your life-style and daily routine, so before you jump into your project be sure to take a close look at your personal realities. If, for instance, you're under pressure at work, or are about to have a new child in the family, or are uncertain about the scope of the project, stand back and consider the situation objectively. You might realize that it's more sensible to tackle just one room instead of the entire first floor, postpone the whole process for a few months, or consult with a professional interior designer after all.

Naturally, the structural limitations of your home can influence the outcome of your design project, too. You may discover that the drafty window you hoped to replace with an insulated version is a more complicated task than you foresaw, or that your plans to alter the layout seem more ambitious than you first anticipated. As is true with a limited budget, however, the limitations of a room can be an opportunity in disguise—a chance for you to reconsider the existing space and come up with creative solutions without needing to remodel at all.

Working With a Professional

Although you may feel perfectly at ease with designing your own spaces, there may be times when you're unsure about a particular decision or feel that you could use some guidance. Perhaps you've discovered that the project is more time-consuming than you had anticipated, or that you need help with reorganizing spaces or figuring out a lighting scheme. Working with an interior designer can make you aware of design possibilities that might not have occurred to you, and—contrary to what you might expect—save you money in the long run.

A well-qualified interior designer brings to the scene not only education and experience in the design of interior spaces but also imagination and a well-trained eye. His or her contacts with the trade—a network of suppliers, manufacturers, and custom shops—and access to the most up-to-date and hard-to-find products can be invaluable in decorating a home. And a competent designer can balance what fits the spaces with what fits your life-style and budget.

Independent Designer

There are several ways to use the talents of a design professional. You might decide to collaborate on a consulting basis at an hourly fee to request help with the initial planning, let's say, or with selecting and ordering furnishings. Fees vary considerably, depending on the designer's experience and reputation, but the hourly rate usually ranges from about $60 to $200. Some designers will agree to consult over three or four sessions for a lump sum, which may amount to fewer dollars per hour.

Another way to use a design professional is on what's called a cost-plus basis: The designer works with you during the entire project, ordering materials and furnishings from the trade at wholesale prices, then marking up the items anywhere from 15 to 35 percent to cover the cost of his or her services. This buying arrangement usually costs you less than retail buying and gives you access to the designer's sources and expertise. There are several variations to the cost-plus theme—the designer might be able to get a large discount on a retail item, for instance, and then charge you a price that's still less than what you'd pay if you bought it at the store yourself. Or, if you can't find the furnishings you want to fit your budget and tastes, the designer can consult an independent custom shop and order precisely what you wish at a more affordable price.

Design Studio

Another way to use the services of a design professional is to take advantage of the full-service design studios offered by some large retail stores. For a nominal fee, as little as $100, the in-house interior designer will consult with you, visit your home, and help with your plans. Naturally, the store hopes that you will purchase most of your furnishings, accessories, lighting fixtures, and so forth from their shelves—and will refund the consulting fee if you do—but if you wish to purchase through showrooms, or wholesale outlets, the designer can order the items for you on a cost-plus basis and mark them up accordingly.

Referral

In most cases, the best way to find an interior designer is through referral: Rather than flip through the Yellow Pages, ask for recommendations. Note the names of designers whose work you've seen at friends' homes, decorator show houses, or in local magazines and newspapers. Call the closest chapter of the American Society of Interior Designers (ASID) for a listing of members in your area. (Some designers are affiliated with the similar International Society of Interior Designers, or ISID.) Membership in these organizations is a fairly accurate sign that the individual is well trained in all aspects of interior design. Some chapters keep files of members, with photographs of their work and information about their areas of special interest.

Have an Interview

When you find the designer who seems to be an ideal match, make an appointment to meet personally and view his or her portfolio. If you decide to work together, be clear about your expectations in terms of time and cost. And if, for whatever reason, your personalities don't mesh or things don't work out, go elsewhere. A second opinion, or another solution, may be just what you and your home need.

On Your Own

If, in the end, you decide to be your own interior designer, you can take a few steps to put yourself in touch with some of the products and services available to the professional. The design centers of most cities offer retail stores intermixed with showrooms open typically only to the trade. Some of these retail outlets are willing to trim their prices to get your business. In addition, furniture showrooms will open their doors on occasion to sell to the public at wholesale prices. You can also watch for ASID sales, at which items bought by interior designers for special projects or to display in their studios are placed up for sale at great savings.

ONE ROOM, THREE WAYS

As you've discovered in this chapter, creating a personal decorating style is a very individual matter, influenced not only by your tastes but also by family composition and budget. To inspire you in your own decorating plans, this section illustrates three different decorating solutions for the same living room.

Planning is the Key

The interior designs of these imaginary rooms have been carefully planned with the ages and activities of family members firmly in mind. The materials and furnishings have been specifically selected to suit the intended use—and users—of the space. Although the environments are quite different in mood and style—and are a reflection of the individuality of each family—they are all visually pleasing, functional, comfortable, and completely livable.

As you look over the illustrations on the following three pages, you'll note that the size, shape, and structure of each room are identical: Measuring about 17 feet by 20 feet, the living room has a fireplace on one wall, two large windows on another wall, an opening into an adjoining room or hall cut into a third wall, and French doors (leading perhaps to a porch, sunroom, or patio) on the fourth wall. None of the decorating plans alters any existing structural features; only the shelving and cabinetry on the fireplace wall have been modified to suit specific storage needs. Cosmetic changes to walls, floors, and windows combine with well-chosen and well-placed furnishings, lighting, and accessories to give the rooms their distinctive personalities.

As you study each room more closely, try to picture the families who use the living space on a day-to-day basis. If you stretch your imagination a little, you might interpret the scenarios in two different ways. In one approach, these living rooms might cater to three distinct families residing in similar houses in the same neighborhood. Each family has the same space to work with but has wide variations in lifestyle, budget, and needs.

Following a different approach, you might think of the illustrations as depicting the same room in the same home as it undergoes decorating changes over the years—initially, when the couple first purchases the house, as an informal family living space; a decade or so later, when the youngsters are older and more independent, as a mostly adult environment; and, finally, after the children have gone off to college or have married, or are otherwise out on their own, as a purely adult retreat intended for formal living and entertaining.

However you decide to visualize the families, many of the steps these imaginary homeowners took in creating a personal style and bringing their projects from concept to fruition are the same ones you will use in your own decorating plans. They had to consider the realities of time, skills, and budget. They thought about maintenance, durability, long-term appearance, and—always—life-style. They took the planning one step at a time, developed a color scheme, researched materials, and spent money only when they were sure they were ready. The following descriptions of each room will give you some insight into the thought process behind each room design.

Dual-Duty and Informal

The professional couple in their early thirties who recently purchased this house have brought ingenuity, a fresh attitude, and lively looks to this all-round living and family space. With two preschoolers in day care, the monthly mortgage to pay, and limited hours and budget to devote to revamping the room, these first-time homeowners decided to make the most of inexpensive and recycled furnishings and reuse items they have owned since their single and early married days. Furthermore, they wanted to create an atmosphere where parents and youngsters could be together and feel at ease with the surroundings.

To meet their family needs, the room required comfortable, flexible seating arrangements; areas for watching TV, listening to music, and playing games; and play spaces that could be expanded or confined, and cleaned up in a jiffy. That meant plenty of storage within a child's reach and a place to keep larger, hard-to-store toys. The parents also needed a room appropriate for adult activities when the children weren't present and dressy enough to host informal get-togethers with friends. They decided to turn the fireplace wall into a focal point, installing bookshelves, repainting the tile surrounding the fireplace and adding a slate hearth, and earmarking a section of the wall system as a small but complete media center.

As the homeowners planned the room, they made a point of selecting materials that were easy to maintain, durable, and affordable. They opted for painted finishes on walls, woodwork, and ceiling; a natural-finish hardwood floor; and sturdy cotton fabrics for furnishings and window coverings. They picked a color scheme built around the primary hues—with an emphasis on blue and red—that is cheerful, youthful without being childish, and easy to live with.

To find furnishings to suit the space, the family spent their weekends scouring garage sales, local antique and second-hand shops, and low-cost import stores. The love seat, armchair, and ottoman were garage-sale bargains, shabby but in good condition: Now covered with easy-care slipcovers sewn from a soil-hiding cotton duck print and a companion striped ticking, the pieces look and function like new. Lightweight canvas director's chairs and floor pillows can be moved around freely to make seating meet the needs of the moment. Storage solutions came from several sources in many shapes and sizes—old barrels, a trunk, boxes, a chest of drawers, and a small cupboard—most given fresh coats of paint. And a trip to the salvage yard unearthed some old door panels that now serve

to screen off a corner play area: Painted, hinged together, and attached to the wall on one edge, the screen can be positioned in a number of ways to provide flexible play space.

The couple accessorized the fireplace wall with a display of majolica plates—bought on their honeymoon in Italy—and hung two favorite posters saved from their previous apartment. They reused the flat-weave dhurrie rug as well, recognizing that its colors and pattern complemented the other objects in the room. Finally, they purchased a new track lighting system to help provide both general and accent lighting, and bought a pair of torchieres to illuminate the game table and the reading area opposite it. The result—a

simple, straightforward, light-hearted room—works for this family on a practical and aesthetic level.

Sophisticated and Semiformal

When redecorating the living room, the owners of this house sought to bring a touch of class to a space that was ordinary in appearance and seldom used. Since the house had a multipurpose family area off the kitchen and a separate dining room, the couple decided to treat this room as a mostly adult living and entertaining space, semiformal in mood, yet outfitted with furnishings and fabrics that would retain their good looks even when the couple's three children and several pets were in attendance.

As added incentive to the decorating plans, the couple had recently inherited some fine older furnishings—a grand piano, a handsome secretary desk, and a large oriental rug. Moreover, on a combined business and pleasure trip to Hong Kong, they had begun collecting Asian art and ceramics, which they desired to display.

In developing the room design, the couple decided to let the colors of the rug form the basis of the overall color scheme—a restful palette of subdued salmons, browns, terra-cotta, and blues—colors that would please the eye and, with practicality in mind, not show the inevitable dog and cat hair. They also planned to invest in some new seating, a versatile sectional sofa and comfortable lounge chair and

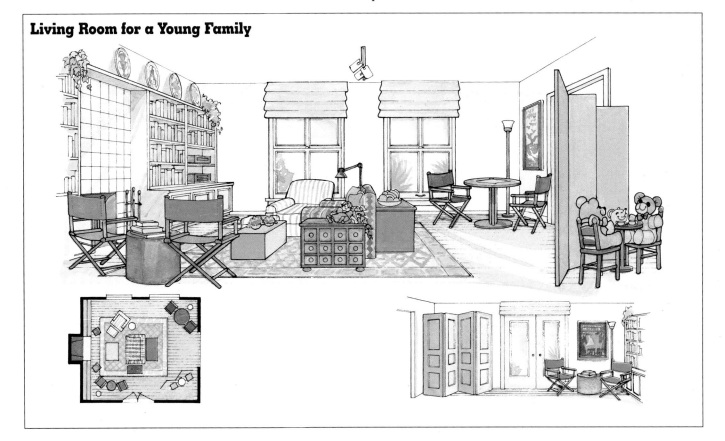

Living Room for a Young Family

ottoman. When selecting fabrics, however, the homeowners consulted with an interior designer to determine the best materials for the job. Together they chose a moderately priced mohair for the sofa upholstery (so durable, said the designer, that it's often used on movie theater seats), with silk pillows for a change of texture, and a wool blend for the chair and ottoman. The designer also suggested the window covering—a heavy, textured fabric allowed to hang loosely for a soft effect.

To underscore the new role of the room as a relaxing adult space, the couple created a library/music area along the fireplace wall, refacing the firebox in slate tile and adding adjustable bookshelves and a pair of cabinets to house the stereo system. Track lighting illuminates the seating area and its surrounding objects, while several floor lamps provide supplemental lighting for reading and playing the piano.

In order to display the couple's art and accessories collected during their travels, and to provide flat surfaces and meet storage needs, they made use of a variety of Japanese *tansus*— chests and boxes traditionally used to store money, medications, and personal items. Two large palms, uplit from behind to dramatize the plants' graceful forms, balance out the corners and add a little greenery.

If you release your imagination and picture this room as the same one encountered in the first scenario, but a decade later, you can see how the family's living patterns and needs have changed over the years. With the birth of another child and the adoption of several pets, the couple may have invested in an addition to the family room or converted the basement into a play area, freeing up the living room for their own use. Their budget may now allow them to purchase some new furnishings and light fixtures. Perhaps the slipcovered love seat and armchair have been moved to the family room, and the dhurrie rug now covers its floor. The director's chairs may sport new canvas seats and live in the bedroom that the older kids share, and the playthings and painted furnishings have found a new home in the youngest child's room.

Eclectic and Elegant

This couple in their late fifties has experienced the mixed blessing of children who've grown up and moved away. No longer plagued with worries about a low-maintenance, high-durability environment and a tight budget, they decided to redo their favorite rooms, beginning with the living room. They also wanted a flexible space that could serve as a formal, but comfortable living and dining room. (The "official" dining room could then become an informal family area for use by visiting children and grandchildren.)

The richness of line, color, pattern, and texture that makes

Living Room for a Growing Family

this multiuse living room notable derives from careful attention to detail, thoughtful choice of materials, and an eclectic approach to furnishings. The woman, an admirer of European antiques, had already purchased four Regency-style chairs for dining and a classic English writing table. Her spouse, on the other hand, favors more modern styles.

In planning their design to suit their individual tastes, they intermixed old and new with a keen eye. The upholstered furnishings, for example, carry simple timeless lines, but the love seat is covered in a traditional floral linen print and the pair of lounge chairs and ottoman in leather. Whereas the table behind the sofa is a Chinese reproduction, the glass coffee table is by a contemporary designer. The rich colors of cabinetry, marble-faced fireplace, woodwork, and moldings are offset by the lighter shades of walls, ceiling, and sisal floor covering. Lighting fixtures were selected with variety in mind: a ceiling track system; table and reading lamps that fit any decor; an antique-base desk lamp; and a pair of modern copper console lamps that hint of Art Nouveau. Even the artwork pleases the couple's diverse tastes—a still life by a contemporary artist and a circa 1820 English animal painting.

The owners didn't forget function in planning their room. The matching console tables, purchased at an estate sale, can be pulled away from the wall and pushed together to form a dining table, accompanied by the antique side chairs. The ample writing table can be drawn into service as a buffet. The couple made the most of the fireplace wall, too. One set of cabinets opens to reveal a compact home office, with computer, pull-out table for keyboard or work space, printer, and storage; the other side of the fireplace holds the media center.

If you return once again to the theme of "same house, same room," and picture this couple twenty-five years or so after they purchased their home, you can appreciate how even a "typical" room can be modified so that its personality keeps step with changing needs and priorities. Now semiretired, without the need to go to a formal workplace, they may have opted to convert a portion of the bookshelf wall into an efficient, well-equipped home office (and replaced the fireplace tile with more elegant marble). They may have relocated the family heirlooms to a different area of the house—bringing the oriental rug and the secretary to their master bedroom and moving the piano into the family room for their grandchildren to enjoy. Perhaps they offered the sectional sofa to a daughter setting up her first apartment. And, knowing how much her husband cherished his lounge chair and ottoman, it's likely the wife had it re-covered in leather to match the new one she bought.

Living Room for a Couple With Grown Children

21

UNDERSTANDING DESIGN PRINCIPLES

In the realm of interior design, certain concepts are often employed to pull a room together, to set up pleasing relationships among various objects in the room, and to create spatial compositions that are visually and emotionally satisfying. This chapter presents a brief overview of these concepts: the abstract principles of unity, scale and proportion, balance, rhythm, and focus, in combination with the more tangible elements of line, form, texture, pattern, and color. The descriptions of these principles and elements are offered not as rules or absolute truths, but rather as suggested guidelines to help you develop your own design.

Strong, repeating vertical lines can make a small space, such as this bedroom, appear larger. The four-poster bed and striped wallpaper emphasize the airy height of the room rather than its limited floor space.

AN OVERVIEW OF DESIGN CONCEPTS

Some rooms, whatever their decorating style, seem to look and feel right. The various objects relate to each other in pleasing ways. Most likely, the overall design of the room has taken into account certain fundamental concepts. Becoming familiar with these concepts can help you compose your own room designs.

Unity

In design terms, unity means that all parts of a room—its layout, furnishings, color scheme, patterns in fabric and wallcoverings—are arranged to create a single, orderly, harmonious effect that's aesthetically pleasing, functions well, and relates comfortably to the rest of the house. The various objects in the room seem to belong and be at home with one another.

Achieving unity doesn't mean that all the colors or patterns have to be the same or perfectly coordinated, or that furnishings must be of the same period or style, but rather that the overall space has a feeling of continuity. Rooms that adjoin each other visually need unity as well, some common characteristic that carries the eye smoothly from one area to the other. Walls might all be painted the same color, flooring wear the same material, windows be covered in similar treatments.

Often a thread of unity is already present in the architecture of a space—characteristics that repeat themselves from room to room, such as moldings, and detailing in windows and doors. Sometimes, unity shows up in smaller ways, too: Dining room chairs might carry the same fabric or color combination as the toss pillows on the living room sofa, or the kitchen wallpaper may coordinate with the pattern on the wing chair in the family room.

A unified look doesn't have to be boring or monotonous. A degree of variety and contrast can create interest and add life without detracting from the overall theme of the room. In fact, an item or two not in complete harmony with the rest of the scheme can introduce excitement—a modern sculpture in an otherwise traditional setting, a boldly colored wall—as long as the major components work together visually and functionally.

Scale and Proportion

In design terms, scale and proportion are closely related. Scale is generally an indication of the size of objects, especially as they relate to each other, to people, and to the spaces they occupy. Proportion is an expression of the comparative relationship between a part (or parts) and the whole. An enormous dining table squeezed into a tiny dining space is out of scale with the size of the room and perhaps out of proportion with the nearby furnishings. A child's chair may look out of scale and lost alongside the living room sofa but perfectly at home in the child's bedroom among smaller objects. That's not to say you can't introduce an object that's out of scale to make a decorative statement. An overstuffed chair can make a small space seem more intimate, or a diminutive chair in the company of standard-sized furnishings can serve as an interesting foil to the eye.

Rooms and their furnishings seem in proper scale when they fit psychologically and physically the people who use them; they seem in good proportion when they express unity and feel balanced. In a successfully decorated room, the seating relates well to the other furnishings and is sized to accommodate the people who use the room; the windows and their coverings seem to take up the right amount of wall space; and the artwork over the fireplace mantel looks just right whether you view it from a sitting or a standing position. Achieving a scale that's appropriate for you and your spaces may take some practice; your intuition can help give you guidance.

Balance

In many ways balance is closely related to scale and proportion. A room in balance has a sense of equilibrium and a feeling that the various areas of the room are evenly weighted. Picturing the way a seesaw works can help you understand balance. If children of about the same size take their places at each end of the seesaw, the board remains balanced. If big brother sits across from little sister, the heavier end won't get off the ground and the lighter end will remain suspended in space. To bring the board back in balance, he can move closer to the center to redistribute the weight, or she can increase the weight on her end with another playmate.

Spaces can be balanced in a similar way. If one side of the room features the architectural focal point or holds most of the furnishings, and the other is relatively bare, you can achieve a balanced effect by giving the "light" side some visual weight. You can treat the wall with a different color and texture or cover it with a boldly patterned paper; you can create a secondary seating area with a small grouping of furnishings, perhaps borrowing one piece from the larger group; you might even give the lighter side of the room importance by hanging artwork on the wall and accenting it with dramatic lighting. Although it's desirable to emphasize the fine architectural features of a room, keeping them in balance with the rest of the space is important, too.

Balance may be symmetrical—when objects of similar weight or design are placed on either side of an axis (or imaginary line) at equal distances from each other. Or, balance may be asymmetrical, when objects that are dissimilar in weight and design are positioned so that they appear to be equidistant from each other. Symmetrical balance is fairly easy to identify because it is orderly—the mantel with the mirror centered directly above, with matching candlesticks of descending height on either side. Symmetrical balance can underscore a room's formality. Asymmetrical balance is more challenging to achieve, often more interesting to experience, and typically less formal in appearance. Here the mantel may still have a mirror (or painting) centered above, but the objects on the shelf may be grouped according to visual weight.

In a third form of balance, radial, objects are arranged in a circular pattern around a center point—seating encircling a round coffee table—again their visual weight distributed to achieve a sense of equilibrium.

Rhythm

More likely than not, if a room has visual unity, a sense of balance, and an overall feeling of continuity, it expresses rhythm as well. Rhythm suggests movement marked by a succession of elements that recur on a regular basis or develop into a pattern—such as tempo in music or dance. Rhythm in design can be achieved through repetition, alternation, or progression. Fabrics and wallcoverings often repeat the same motifs or patterns to set up a kind of rhythm; windows of varying sizes may alternate around a room or within a house; furniture arrangements may include pieces that progress in size from small to large; a grouping

Repetition of shapes, such as the orchids on the table, the chair backs, and the windows, gives this subtly colored dining room unity and balance.

Two powerful focal points—a beautiful fireplace and stunning bay view—vie for attention in this formal library. By arranging the chairs at an angle, both can be enjoyed.

of plants may progress in height from low in the foreground to high near the wall.

Sometimes, rhythm is so apparent visually that it gives the impression that you are seeing balance at work, as when all the prints on a wall are the same size and are framed in exactly the same manner. Like balance, rhythm can be subtle, too. When the eye flows easily around a room, settling first on one object or grouping to take it in, then traveling to a second point of interest, then another,

it is experiencing the rhythm of the space.

Contrast can be an effective way to keep the repetitive or progressive patterns of rhythm from becoming visually monotonous or, at the other extreme, confusing or distracting. A deliberate contrast can create a welcome visual resting point, interject surprise, or act as a counterpoint without detracting from the overall continuity of the design.

Focus

Giving a room focus, or emphasis, can bring vitality to its spaces and create a center of interest that attracts the eye and holds its attention. The emphasis might be on a single focal point—an architectural feature such as a fireplace or a bay window, or a prominent object such as a grand piano. Sometimes, the center of interest can be a dominant grouping of furniture, or a captivating collection of artwork.

Emphasizing some aspects of a room to create a single point of interest usually calls for de-emphasizing others according to their relative importance. A fireplace mantel that's intended as a focal point should be emphasized almost as much as the fireplace itself. Nearby seating can enhance the area around the point of interest by acting as a secondary emphasis that contributes to the focus of the room without competing with it. De-emphasizing can be almost as valuable a tool in designing spaces as establishing a focus. It can provide a noncompetitive background for the areas of emphasis and can also keep the eye from noticing an architectural flaw or a part of the room that doesn't warrant attention.

Occasionally, a room may have two or three focal points that all merit emphasis—a handsome fireplace, a stunning view, perhaps a wall of finely crafted cabinetry. Giving them equal weight may take careful planning. It may be easier to give each a place of prominence in the room by emphasizing one somewhat more than the others.

Line and Form

We seldom give line and form much thought because they are so much a part of daily experience, but as design elements they can influence the way a room looks and feels almost as much as color. Lines, whether straight or curved, can be assembled to represent a shape such as a rectangle or an oval. When given structure and substance, shapes become forms—a chair, let's say, or a chandelier. Rooms are usually thought of in terms of shape, and the objects in them by their forms.

Lines can be highly expressive in the design of a room. Vertical lines and forms are often associated with strength, support, energy, and upward movement (walls, mountains, the standing or walking human figure). Horizontal lines and forms suggest less direct movement—sideways energy—and more relaxing images (the horizon, a person at rest with his or her feet propped up on the sofa).

Interior spaces that emphasize the vertical with high ceilings, tall windows and doors, and upright furniture tend to feel somewhat formal and impersonal, sometimes lofty and dramatic. Those that underscore the horizontal with low ceilings, broad window and door openings, and stretched-out furnishings seem more intimate, warmer, less formal, occasionally claustrophobic. Typically, people are most comfortable when ceilings are neither too high nor too low, and when horizontal and vertical lines are kept in balance and suit the human scale.

You can add an illusion of height and formality to a low-ceilinged room by playing up the vertical dimensions: striped wallcoverings, window treatments that extend to the floor, tall bookshelves, indoor trees. Likewise, a room that needs visual broadening can benefit from baseboards, moldings, and wallpaper borders that carry the eye around the room perimeter, and from plump seating, tables, and other flat surfaces that accentuate the horizontal.

Diagonal lines evoke curiosity and suggest activity. They are most effective when they lead to a stopping point that doesn't leave the eye stranded in space—a sloping ceiling rising to a peak, for instance, or a collection of pictures stepped with the stairs to the second floor. Curved lines and forms can soften a room that seems stiff or confining, though too many curves may make a person feel restless and confused. Just the presence of an oval table, a gently contoured sofa, or a round-backed chair can make an angular furniture grouping more inviting. Many classic furnishings—those that fit and function beautifully in almost any style of room—are curvilinear in form, blending the best of both curved and straight lines.

Texture and Pattern

Texture refers to the surface quality of materials and objects—how they look and feel—and is often perceived as rough or smooth, hard or soft. The way a texture actually feels, its tactile quality, influences its use in a room design to a certain degree. Very rough, uneven surfaces are uncomfortable to sit on and may be difficult to walk across; but a rough plastered wall or a coarse woven tapestry may feel interesting and satisfying to the touch. The visual quality of textures, their appearance, can greatly influence the composition of a room. A smooth wall can be given the appearance of having an uneven surface with a patterned wallpaper or the application of a faux finish—or be made to look even smoother covered with a shiny material that reflects light, such as high-gloss paint or satin fabric.

Sometimes, texture is in the material itself, as in the grain and knots of wood, or comes from the way an object was made. Sometimes, it results from applying one material over another to achieve a special effect—etching designs in glass or sewing piping around cushions.

Pattern refers to the decoration of two-dimensional objects, such as wallcoverings and fabric, and is an important visual element in the design of a room. Most patterns have a definite rhythm to their lines, whether they draw their inspiration from nature, the abstract world, or stylistic themes—simplified versions of conventional subjects. Ornament is closely related to both pattern and texture because it has to do with the enrichment of a surface, whether it's applied or is an integral part of the design.

COLOR BASICS

The eye distinguishes countless colors— millions perhaps—all based on gradations of what appears in the rainbow, all variations of the primary colors, red, yellow, and blue.

The Color Wheel

When light waves of a certain length stimulate the eye, it interprets them as a particular color. Daylight is the random mixture of all light in all its wavelengths; when daylight passes through a prism (or a raindrop), it breaks down into a spectrum of colors (or a rainbow) that ranges from red at one end, through orange, yellow, green, and blue, to violet at the other. When this band of color is bent into a circle, it forms the color wheel. From a decorating standpoint, the color wheel can be a useful tool to help see how different colors relate to each other and how they can be combined to create a pleasing palette for the home.

The color wheel illustrated on the opposite page is divided into 12 sections, representing the primary, secondary, and tertiary colors of the spectrum. Red, yellow, and blue are considered primary colors because they are fundamental—not mixed from others but rather the base from which all others are derived. The secondary colors—orange, green, and violet—are each made from equal amounts of the primaries on either side. Lastly, the six

tertiaries, red-orange and blue-violet among them, are derived from equal amounts of their neighbors. By varying the proportions of these colors—adding a little or a lot more of a neighbor, for instance—you can create any number of new colors, or hues, and give each a name.

Hue

Simply described, the term *hue* refers to the name assigned to a particular color; it is often used interchangeably with the word *color.* Some hues carry universally accepted names, such as red or blue-green, as found on the color wheel. But many hues are arbitrarily assigned: Some can be fairly easy to recognize—lilac, for example, or apricot—but others can be difficult to interpret because the name suggests so many possibilities. In the family of blues, for instance, sky, slate, marine, and periwinkle evoke images that have different color meanings to you, your spouse, the carpet manufacturer, and the paint dealer.

Analogous Hues

Related, or analogous, hues are found next to each other on the color wheel and typically share a common primary base: Orange-yellow, yellow, and

yellow-green are analogous, as are yellow, yellow-green, and green, since all share the same primary. Because they have something in common, analogous hues can make for a harmonious family of color.

Complementary Hues

Hues found directly opposite each other on the wheel are called complementary. Typically they set up a strong contrast when placed together— orange and blue, for instance, or red-violet and yellow-green. When one of the complements is lightened with white, darkened with black, or toned down with gray, the pair can coexist more harmoniously. Analogous and complementary hues will be covered more fully in the section on color schemes (page 46).

Value

The relative lightness or darkness of a color is its value. Any hue can be lightened with the addition of white in large or small amounts, and becomes a tint. When darkened with the addition of black, it is called a shade. The variations can be dramatic: Any hue can be lightened (or darkened) so much that its color is barely noticeable unless positioned against white (or black). Pink is a tint of red that typically has a moderate amount of white added to

create a strong pastel; cream is a tint of yellow containing comparatively more white. Olive is a shade of green that's been darkened moderately; navy is a shade of blue containing a larger amount of black.

Tone

Hues with some gray added, rather than just white or black, are referred to as tones. If lavender is a tint of violet, then mauve might be considered a tone. Many colors with a smoky effect are hues that have been toned down with a moderate amount of gray.

Value Scale

The value scale shown on the opposite page is another useful tool in color planning because it demonstrates some of the variations in value you might expect to see between the lightest tint and the darkest shade of any number of hues. This particular scale shows variations between white and black. The topmost square is almost white; the bottom one, nearly solid black. The midpoint is a middle-value gray. The small circle in the center of each square carries the same middle-value gray. As you look at the scale, you'll note that the color of the circle seems to change, appearing quite dark in comparison to the lightest tint, almost white in relation to the darkest shade. Toward the center, where the contrast in value is less extreme, the difference is also much less apparent.

Understanding Color

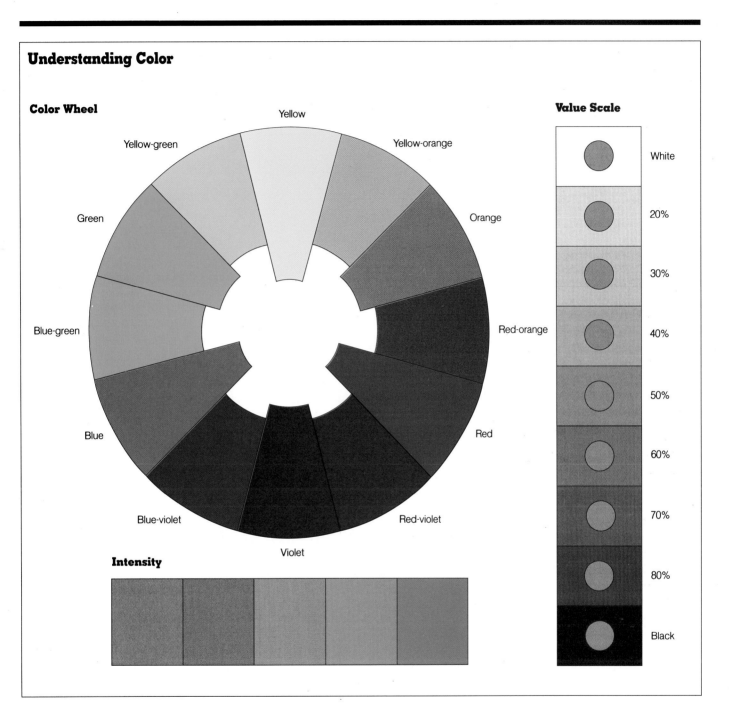

Color Wheel

Yellow
Yellow-green
Yellow-orange
Green
Orange
Blue-green
Red-orange
Blue
Red
Blue-violet
Red-violet
Violet

Intensity

Value Scale

White
20%
30%
40%
50%
60%
70%
80%
Black

Intensity

Another characteristic of color is intensity (sometimes referred to as chroma), which indicates the strength and brightness of a hue, undiluted by tinting or shading. (You might think of it as the color straight from the artist's tube.) The more of the dominant hue, and the less tint or shade, the more vivid and intense the color appears to the eye. Royal blue and royal purple are familiar hues that can be described as intense, ideal perhaps for a monarch's robe but probably better in smaller doses in the rooms of your home.

A strong hue can look more intense and even seem jarring to the eye if placed next to an equally intense complement. The combinations of bright blue and orange, or pure red and green, better suit flags and football uniforms than the walls of your room. Pairing an intense color with a tint or a shade of its complement, however, can make a satisfactory combination—bright red Christmas ornaments against a dark green tree, or a peach tint background enlivened with accents of a strong blue.

COLOR, LIGHT, AND MOOD

Without light, there is no color, so it's not surprising that even subtle changes in lighting influence the way colors appear. Sometimes, the connection between color and emotion is subtle, even unconscious, but it influences the way you feel and can even affect your physical well-being.

Light Affects Color

Choose a wall in your home and think about the way it looks when sunlight strikes the surface. Think of its appearance in the morning, at noon, and at night when the lights are on. Does daylight produce glare, or artificial light cloak the walls in garish tones? If you understand the interaction of light and color, you can plan for a satisfying result.

Natural Light

Since daylight contains all the colors of the spectrum, it is in natural light that colors appear in their truest form—and at midday that they take on their purest appearance.

Light from the north tends to be cool and steady, toward the blue end of the spectrum. Eastern light looks bright and yellow in the early morning but evens out as the day passes. Light from the south nearly always looks and feels warm—an especially welcome attribute during winter months—and can seem warmer still as it moves west and takes on the reddish cast of late afternoon.

Artificial Light

The quality of light—and color—changes substantially in the presence of artificial light-ing, which also contains the colors of the spectrum but in proportions different from daylight. The incandescent bulbs typically used in home lighting give off a yellowish cast: They can bathe a warm-hued room in a golden glow, but they can turn even intense colors from the cool end of the spectrum dull and lifeless. Fluorescent bulbs commonly found in kitchens usually emit a cool blue or green cast that can perk up the look of salad greens but make a tomato or a red pepper appear somewhat gray; when turned on strong, some fluorescents can turn even the richest of warm hues murky. Halogen lamps, which offer a

Crisp white walls and upholstery and gleaming wood floors are brightened by natural light streaming through the shuttered windows.

clear white light with little color distortion, passably approximate natural light; energy efficient but still comparatively expensive, halogens are gaining in popularity because they show off colors in their almost-true form.

Color Affects Mood

If you've ever felt "blue" or predicted an outcome to be "rosy," or donned a yellow shirt to cheer yourself up, you know that color has an impact on your emotions. Consequently, the colors you select for your home must not only look right to your eye but feel right as well. Furthermore, the time of the day and quality of light will change the way color feels—yellow will look and feel duller and darker at dusk than in broad daylight.

Red, Orange, Yellow

Although response to color is a personal thing, researchers have learned that certain colors tend to elicit certain emotions. Red, for instance, associated with heat and fire, usually quickens the pulse and raises body temperature. Because red energizes and stimulates, it might be a good choice for an exercise room, but not for the bedroom of a hyperactive child. Orange shares some of the energizing qualities of red and is thought to stimulate the appetite. Though you probably don't want to paint your kitchen an intense orange, a peachy tint might do nicely. Yellow is associated with sunshine and cheerfulness; it feels bright

rather than stimulating and has been noted to increase creativity in people. Yellow is a versatile decorating color because in its pale tints it becomes almost neutral in effect. Red, orange, and yellow—and their variations on the color wheel—are considered warm hues.

Green, Blue, Violet

Psychologically speaking, green is perceived as calming and relaxing—like the greenery of a garden. Coloring a room

in tints and shades of green can help you wind down, achieve serenity, and, when warmed with a little red or orange, give you a fresh outlook on matters. Blue also has a restful effect and, like water, can suggest coolness and calm. A soothing blue can help a south-facing room feel cooler, or a bedroom more conducive to sleeping, but if used in too dark a shade can make any room feel cold and gloomy. Not surprisingly, green and blue—and, to a

lesser degree, violet—are considered cool hues.

Violet, or purple (which is really an intense version of violet), can be a difficult color to decorate with, in part because it straddles the line between cool blue and warm red; it can feel either warm or cool depending on the light, the other hues in the room, and your own moods. However, violet is associated with promoting self-expression and one's artistic side and can be an effective decorating color with thoughtful planning.

Blue is a good choice for a child's room. The right blue—not too bright or too dark—creates a restful, soothing mood. Accent pillows and trim on windows and furniture add some contrast to the primary color of the room.

PLANNING YOUR SPACES

Now that you've considered some of the looks and styles that might fit into your decorating program, have examined your family life-style, and have thought about your budget and personal needs, the next step is to begin planning your design project. Even if you're doing just one room, deciding how you'll divide, rearrange, and furnish the spaces and how you will use color will take some time and additional thought, both well worth the effort to get the results you want. Planning your approach on paper first gives you the flexibility to experiment with many possibilities before making up your mind.

A room can undergo a dramatic face-lift even without structural changes. This delightful living room bears no resemblance to its uninspired former self, yet the transformation is only cosmetic.

MAKING SPACE WORK

Commonly, rooms that function poorly are prime candidates for refurbishing because they fail to meet specific physical needs. Sometimes, however, rooms that fail to meet psychological needs can be candidates, too. It's important to examine the space you have. If it isn't working for you, it's time to rethink its use.

Planning for Your Needs

Sometimes, a design project comes into being because your home simply needs a face-lift or an update to make it look its best. Most of the time, though, there's a more compelling reason for a change. Perhaps you've just moved into a larger house and your old furnishings are inadequate, worn out, and at odds with the way your family functions. Maybe your family has increased in size and you need to reorganize the children's spaces. Perhaps the spare bedroom is such a hodge-podge that it can't function for work, study, or leisure. Or, you may give priority to redoing a room that matters because, let's say, it's the heart of your home, even though other parts of the house are in worse physical condition or not as functional as you'd like.

Bubble Diagrams

One exercise to help you weigh your various physical and psychological needs and put them in perspective is to draw a bubble diagram of your home—a freehand graphic picture of the way the rooms relate to each other, not so much in terms of

literal size but rather in their relative importance to family living patterns and daily use. The largest bubbles signify the most important rooms, the smallest the least. Arrows or lines can be employed to show rooms that are connected physically; the thicker the line, the greater the traffic between those rooms.

For instance, the family room may be the most important room in your home, although not the largest by far, because it's the hub of family activity and the place where even guests gather. The problem, however, is that the space isn't really big enough to accommodate a comfortable sitting area and it doesn't have access to the ever-popular rear deck. By contrast, let's say that the seldom-used living-dining room has plenty of space and opens to the deck, but gets little activity except as a route to the outdoors and to host an occasional dinner party.

Drawing simple bubble diagrams can help you look at several potential solutions to the problem that don't involve remodeling. You might, for instance, realize that the best solution is to look at your living spaces in an entirely new way. With relatively minor changes, you might convert the living

Using Bubble Diagrams
Existing Floor Plan

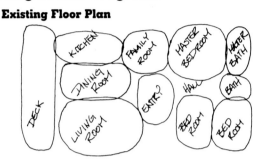

Room Sizes in Terms of Use and Needs (Not Actual Size)

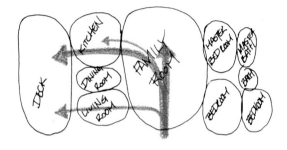

Existing Floor Plan With Room Usage Changed

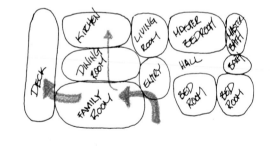

room into the new family center, gaining enough space for a roomy, informal entertaining area both indoors and on the deck, and let the old family room become a more flexible space that could serve as a formal living and dining area, and perhaps also as a library.

Taking part in this exercise can be invaluable in sizing up a house that you may be thinking

of buying to help you see its potential—or reveal its flaws. Bubble diagrams can be helpful, too, in rethinking the makeup of rooms themselves—the relative importance of areas within the room and the ways that family members circulate between them. Most of all, this tool can help you decide which rooms come first in your decorating plans and which changes will meet your needs most adequately.

Composition of Spaces

Planning your spaces to be functional and livable will progress more smoothly if you examine the concept of space as it relates to your own home. Space itself is usually defined by the planes that enclose it—walls, floor, and ceiling—and may be observed as primarily horizontal or vertical. In most houses horizontal and vertical spaces are kept in balance and are designed to fit the human scale. Floor plans are valuable aids in spatial planning because they document the actual size and shape of the area in question and help determine just how much space is available to work with.

Real and Implied Space

The actual size of a room may take on different meaning when you consider both its real and implied spaces. Implied space is an important part of planning because it centers on how the eye perceives space rather than what is actually there. A room with a small floor area, for instance, will seem larger if all surfaces are painted in a light color, partly because the eye travels around the space without interruption and also because the surfaces themselves appear to recede. A small space will also seem larger if it has large windows that frame views and also high ceilings, which give a sense of volume.

Open and Closed Plans

Generally speaking, a floor plan may be described as open, where most functions occur in basically one large space; or closed, where activities take place in a series of separate rooms. In an open plan, which is more typical of contemporary interiors, living spaces flow into one another, often divided by partitions rather than walls. In a closed plan, a more traditional layout prevails, where each room has an assigned name and function. Most homes today offer a combination of open and closed spaces, a mixture of public, social areas and private rooms—open-plan great rooms and kitchen-family areas, for instance, balanced against closed-off bedrooms and baths.

Circulation

Patterns of circulation tend to be different in each type of floor plan. With few walls, and even fewer halls, in an open plan, traffic can go any which way. The challenge is to channel the flow so that the paths are not haphazard but still move freely. Grouping furniture, adding partial walls, and using plants as dividers can be effective means of directing traffic along the most satisfactory routes. A closed plan can create the opposite situation: tight, often congested, traffic paths that overuse some parts of the house (hallways, for example) and underuse others. Sometimes, simply rearranging furniture or reassigning a function of a room can redistribute foot traffic for better flow.

Yet another look at your bubble diagram can give you some hints as to the circulation patterns around your house and within its rooms. You might even have family members pencil in their own paths from morning to night to see how they overlap. Would a change in the function of a room help ease congestion? Would rearranging the furnishings create a short, more direct path to a room that currently requires a long, circuitous route? You might also discover that partially enclosing a too-open plan with a visual divider, such as plants or a folding screen, is just what your living spaces need to function more smoothly.

Manipulating Space

Having enough actual usable space, or the right distribution of space, is the aim of virtually every homeowner. One of the main goals of good planning is learning ways to manipulate space to meet family needs. Finding additional space is sometimes simpler than you might expect; for example, converting an oversized upstairs hall into a multiuse area for sewing, hobbies, and exercise; reworking an attic full of cast-offs into a hideaway, study center, or home office.

A fresh, imaginative point of view can help transform what you've thought of as spatial limitations into opportunities. Planning your spaces in order to make them work for you takes time and thought, but it is a necessary process to help you get the best results in terms of looks and function, and to be in tune with your life-style and budget.

In an open floor plan, rooms flow into one another.

DOCUMENTING YOUR EXISTING SPACES

This part of the design process is best approached in a step-by-step manner, beginning with an accurate floor plan of your existing spaces and gradually working toward a final layout and furniture plan.

Making a Floor Plan

Most of this phase of the planning process takes place on paper. Drawing a floor plan is a far more efficient and useful technique than actually moving furnishings in and out, or attempting to rearrange spaces. Before you pick up a pencil, though, there are a few preliminary steps to complete. The first is to take photographs of your existing room or rooms from several angles to use for reference as your plans take shape. Next, start a planning binder to hold your bubble diagrams, photographs, and all the plans you'll be developing in this chapter. You might purchase a cardboard file box to store the files on styles, objects, and so forth that you've already started, the planning binder, and any future files. Finally, make up a planning box to hold the various implements you'll need to draw your plans.

Drawing the Floor Plan

A floor plan is a flat, two-dimensional diagram of space, which, to be useful in planning, must be drawn accurately to show the exact proportions and location of structural elements such as walls and doors, and features such as fireplaces, radiators, built-in bookcases, and so forth. Floor plans are always drawn to scale so that the elements of the room represented on paper have the same relative size as the actual elements. For convenience, plans are typically drawn to a scale in which ¼ inch represents 1 foot (though for planning such spaces as bathrooms and kitchens, ½ inch or even 1 inch to the foot is often recommended).

To start, make a rough sketch of the floor plan to use for reference as you measure the room. Indicate any permanent features, such as doors, windows, electrical outlets, phone and TV jacks, and heat registers, even if they are not at floor level. Mark the direction that doors and windows swing.

Using a yardstick or a retractable measuring tape, work your way around the perimeter of the room, preferably on the floor, where it's easier to get an accurate reading, measuring all walls and wall segments, including any jogs. On the rough sketch jot down each measurement as you take it. Go back and measure across the room, wall to wall, in both directions. Check that individual wall segments add up correctly. Note the widths of window and door openings and their frames, and measure the width of the door swing. Mark any features that protrude into the room, such as wall cabinets or the fireplace mantel. Where possible, measure the depth of walls, in case rewiring or altering the plumbing becomes necessary in reworking your spaces.

Now, make a correctly scaled drawing of the same plan. You can make photocopies of the grid provided on page 38, on which ¼ inch equals 1 foot (you'll need five copies in all; heavy-weight paper is recommended); you can purchase a pad of graph paper; or—if you want a larger scale to work with—you can make your own grid. Carefully transfer all the information from your rough sketch to the grid with a pencil and ruler, using the adjustable triangle to help get angles and corners just right. When you have everything accurately in place, finalize your drawing with a narrow-tip felt pen. (If you tape pennies on the underside of the ruler, and hold the pen barrel against its edge, you can avoid smearing the ink.)

Planning Tools

- notebook for making rough sketches and jotting down measurements
- 25-foot retractable tape measure
- grid work sheet or graph paper
- heavy-weight or construction paper
- tissue or tracing paper
- sharp pencils or mechanical pencil
- 12-inch or 18-inch ruler
- adjustable triangle (available at most stationery stores)
- narrow-tip felt pen
- furniture template
- a few crayons
- scissors

Floor Plan of Empty Room

Rough Sketch

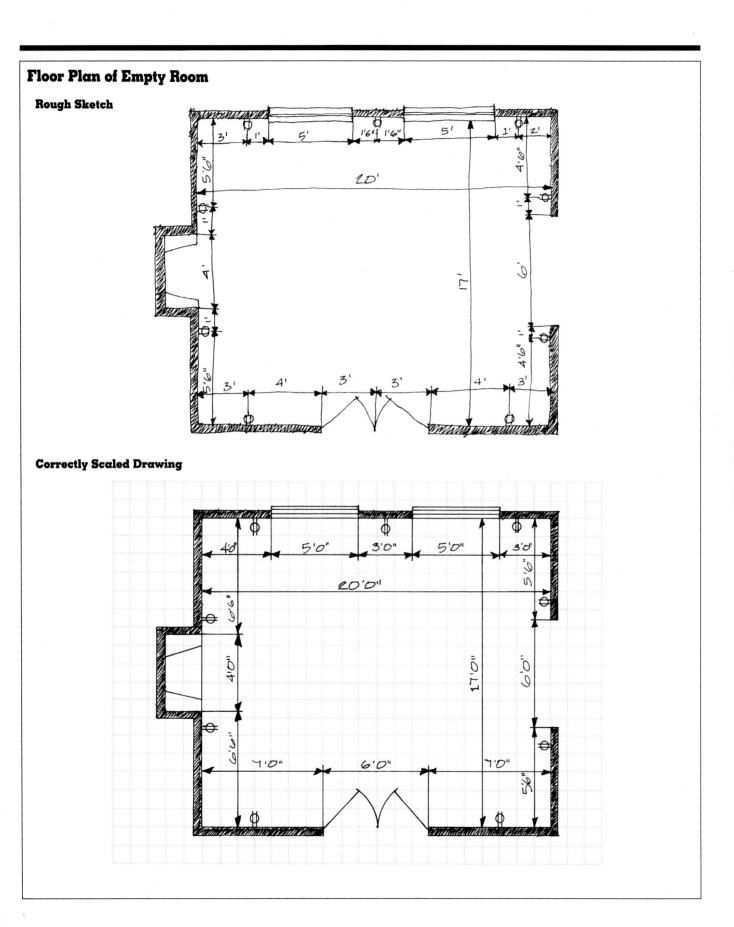

Correctly Scaled Drawing

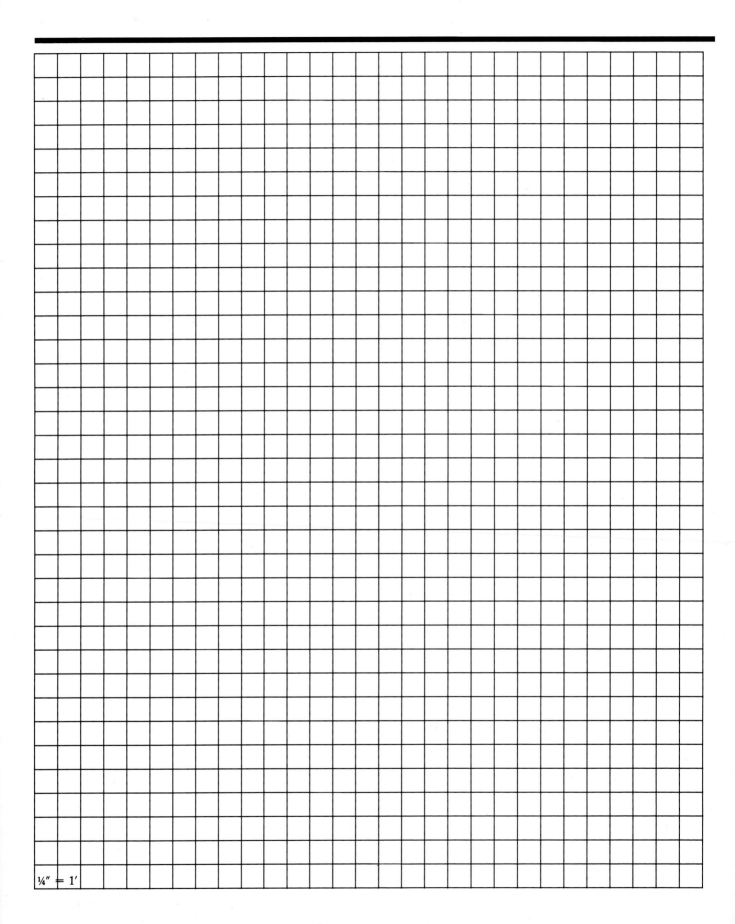

¼″ = 1′

Floor Plan With Wall Elevations

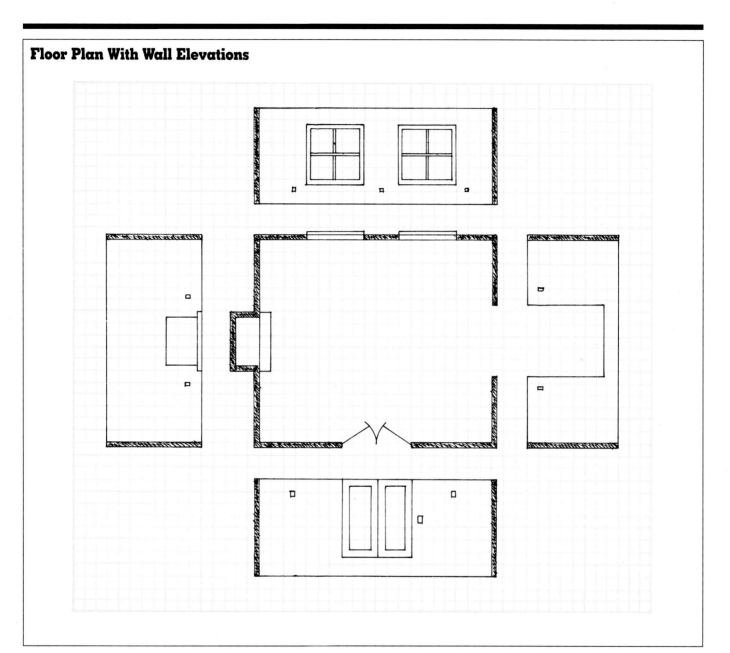

Elevations

An elevation is simply a detailed drawing of each wall, a plan of the vertical dimensions of the room. Elevations give additional information that's helpful in planning the overall spaces of the room and will be useful later when you need to calculate quantities of paint or rolls of wallcovering.

To draw your elevations, follow the same process you did for the floor plan. Start with a rough sketch composed of four boxes, one to represent each wall. Taking one wall at a time, measure its vertical dimension and the height of doors, windows, the fireplace, and so on, remembering such details as baseboards, moldings, and door and window frames. If a wall has a corner shelf or a cabinet that projects into the room, be sure to indicate it on the elevation for the adjoining wall. Do not include furnishings unless they are permanently attached. You already have most of the horizontal measurements on your floor plan, so you can just jot them down without remeasuring—unless you want to check again for accuracy.

Using four separate pieces of grid/graph paper, and exactly the same scale you did for the floor plan, transfer your measurements for each wall to its own sheet. Follow the same procedure, beginning with pencil and finalizing with pen. If you drew your floor plan on a large enough piece of grid/graph paper, put all four wall elevations on the same paper as the floor plan. Or, tape the four elevation sheets to the floor plan, then have a copy service prepare a single, reduced-size photocopy of floor plan with elevations.

Evaluating the Floor Plan

Now that your floor plan and elevations are complete, it's time to make tissue, or tracing paper, overlays. Using overlays atop your drawings affords tremendous flexibility in studying traffic patterns and evaluating what works and what doesn't in your present plan.

Studying the Basic Room

First, place a piece of tissue over the floor plan. Roughly trace the perimeter of the room, marking the doors, and sketch in the shapes of your existing furnishings in their current arrangement. Make photocopies of the tissue and ask family members to draw in their walking patterns around and through the room. (Or you can give everyone a different-color pencil and ask them to document their paths on the original piece of tissue.)

This exercise will give you clues as to what's amiss with your furnishings or their placement or show you the areas that are overused as well as the underutilized spots.

Analyzing Your Furnishings

Next, make decisions about your existing furnishings. What will you keep, and what will you weed out? Are some of your furnishings an obstacle to accomplishing your design goal, or no longer practical for the space? It may help the decision-making process to prepare a room profile sheet similar to the example on the opposite page to assist in analyzing your needs for the room.

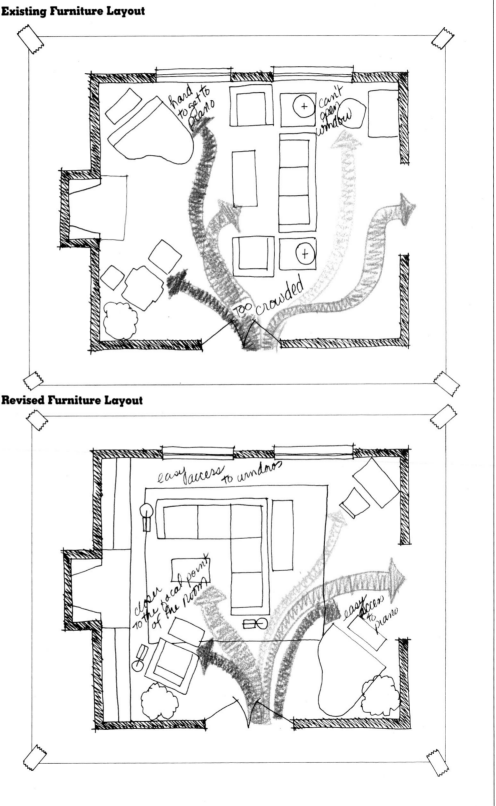

Traffic Patterns

Existing Furniture Layout

hard to get to piano

can't open window

too crowded

Revised Furniture Layout

easy access to windows

closer to the focal point of the room

easy access to piano

Making a Room Profile Sheet

Putting together a brief profile of the room you're planning to redo can help clarify the various steps involved, and also help you keep tabs on what you intend to refurbish or buy anew. Additionally, a profile sheet can be an especially useful tool in documenting expenditures, large and small. You can organize the sheet so that one side carries the headings shown in the example on this page, while the reverse side (or a second sheet) covers the following additional subjects.

• Necessary room repairs and their anticipated costs.

• Professional services needed (such as hiring an electrician to install track lighting or a mason to reface the fireplace) and their estimated costs.

• Refurbishing costs, if any (cleaning the carpets, for instance, or having a chair reupholstered).

• Actual materials and finishes selected for floor, ceiling, walls, and windows, and their respective costs.

• Items purchased or to be purchased, including essential furnishings, secondary items, lighting fixtures, accessories. For each item, record its source, budgeted cost, order and delivery dates, and actual costs.

Naturally, you won't be able to fill in all the information at this stage of your project—such as specific materials and their exact costs—but you can get started. You can store the worksheet in your binder and add to it as you continue to develop your design.

ROOM PROFILE FOR _Living Room_

PRESENT FUNCTION/USERS _Seldom used now that we have a family room. Ordinary looking, lifeless - needs some pizzaz! Do entertain friends here, but I'm embarrassed at worn & shabby sofa and chair. Present furniture arrangement causes awkward traffic flow._

INTENDED FUNCTIONS/USERS _Primarily desire a mostly adult space for our own enjoyment (music, reading, conversation) and for entertaining informally. Also want room to be comfortable for the three kids (and pets of course!) when they want to join us. That means attractive and durable fabrics and colors that won't show dirt._

POSITIVE FEATURES/PROBLEMS _We like the fireplace wall-could be the focal point with more shelving and perhaps a new face around fireplace. French door a nice feature too. More color on the patio would be nice (containers with flowers?) Hardwood floor in good shape._
Problems: Not enough storage! Lighting - inadequate need track system and more lamps. Window view of house next door—need covering to give privacy. Also walls require repair before repainting.

DECORATIVE STYLE/COLOR SCHEME _Semi-formal: sophisticated but not stuffy. Desire an eclectic style so I can intermix the traditional pieces we've inherited with some new seating and our Asian art accessories._
Color scheme: mainly monochromatic. Walls & ceiling off whites in creamy direction. Really like subtle "desert" hues—pale salmon, tan, light gray, reddish browns (not too strong). Plan to use Oriental rug to help select exact shades. Maybe punctuate with blue (toss pillows, glazed ceramic pots?).

ITEMS INTENDING TO REUSE _Family pieces from Mom & Dad: grand piano and bench; antique secretary; Oriental rug (needs cleaning!) Stereo system. Reading lamps. Wood chests (tansus) and woven basket (use as coffee table?) Accessories, pets, artwork, etc._

ITEMS PLANNING TO PURCHASE _New: Seating probably modular. Lounge chair and ottoman, track lighting and additional reading lamps. Large plants (perhaps some flowers and containers for patio). Toss pillows. Window coverings and hardware (but what exactly? I think I may consult an interior designer for advice on fabrics._
Antique or used: Side chair to place by secretary. Additional tansus for storage and table-top surfaces.

CREATING A NEW PLAN

The floor plan and elevations portray your spaces as they are right now. The next step is to revise the space and the furnishings it contains to better suit your needs.

Making a Furniture Plan

As you consider how you might change the composition of the spaces of your room and the placement of its furnishings, there are a few important points to keep in mind. The focus of the plan should always revolve around the primary function of the room and the features and items that support it. The plan should also address the other functions of the room but not be dominated by them. And the final plan must allow for easy, unobstructed movement to permit the intended activities to take place.

Furniture

Once again, planning on paper is the most efficient method to experiment with arranging your present and future furnishings. You can use the furniture templates provided on page 44, making photocopies on heavy-weight paper, or fabricate your own paper or cardboard pieces. Be certain that the width and length of the furnishings depicted are accurate in measurement and drawn

to the same scale as your floor plan. If you do copy these templates, find the shapes that correspond in size to the furnishings you intend to keep, cut them out, and color them for easy identification.

On your floor plan, intermix the furnishings you intend to buy with the existing ones. Position the larger pieces first, then the smaller items. Move the shapes around until you find an arrangement that seems to work (remember design elements such as scale and proportion, balance and focal point, as you work out your arrangement). Carefully lay a piece of tissue on top of your plan and trace the outlines of the room and furnishings. To be certain that you've left enough space to open drawers and doors, lower a drop-down desk, or add a leaf to the table, indicate the area that the opened items will occupy with a dotted line. (Open drawers need two thirds the width of the piece; furniture doors usually require the full width.) Also, be sure you've allowed enough space around and between furnishings for people to walk behind them, sit comfortably, reach forward, and so forth. See page 45 for illustrations of some common clearances.

Traffic Patterns

When your sketch is complete, pencil in the traffic patterns based on the tissues sketched by you and other family members. Are there areas where the flow is too heavy, congested, or awkward? Can you make simple changes in your arrangement to alleviate the situation? Experiment with several different arrangements, trying various sizes and shapes of furnishings. You might discover that two love seats work better than a conventional sofa and an armchair, that modular furnishings offer the flexibility your room needs, that a built-in banquette is a smarter choice for the breakfast nook than a freestanding table and chairs. Make a tissue copy of every layout that has potential as your final plan, examining the traffic flow in each. Save all your tissue copies in your planning binder.

Use Elevations

The elevations that you've drawn can also be helpful in determining your furniture plan, because viewing the vertical dimension can help you see the way the walls will look with furnishings against them or nearby. For instance, on the floor plan you may have positioned a sofa against one wall with tables on either side. When you see them in place on the elevation, however, their proportions may look all

wrong for the length and height of the wall. Or, you may have an uninteresting small window with an even worse view. With a tissue overlay, you can experiment with solutions to the problem window, blocking it with a tall bookcase or built-in cabinetry, or perhaps covering the opening with a painting or stained glass. Elevations can be especially useful to help picture the way a wall will really look when the bookcase is in place or your favorite collection of photographs is arranged on the wall.

Creating a Final Layout

As you consider the various furniture plans you've developed, evaluate each in light of the intended functions of the room and your living patterns. Are your furnishings flexible enough to adapt to extra or future functions? Will they mesh with your life-style? If the room is to be used some of the time for conversing, is seating arranged at comfortable distances to allow normal conversation? If the room has a television or a computer, is the screen positioned so that light doesn't reflect on it? If you've included an entertainment center, is it outfitted to hold larger or different equipment in the future? As you arranged furnishings on the floor plan, did you consider natural light and views? How about lamps and fixtures for reading and illuminating the room at night? Does circulation around objects and through spaces flow smoothly?

Final Furniture Layout

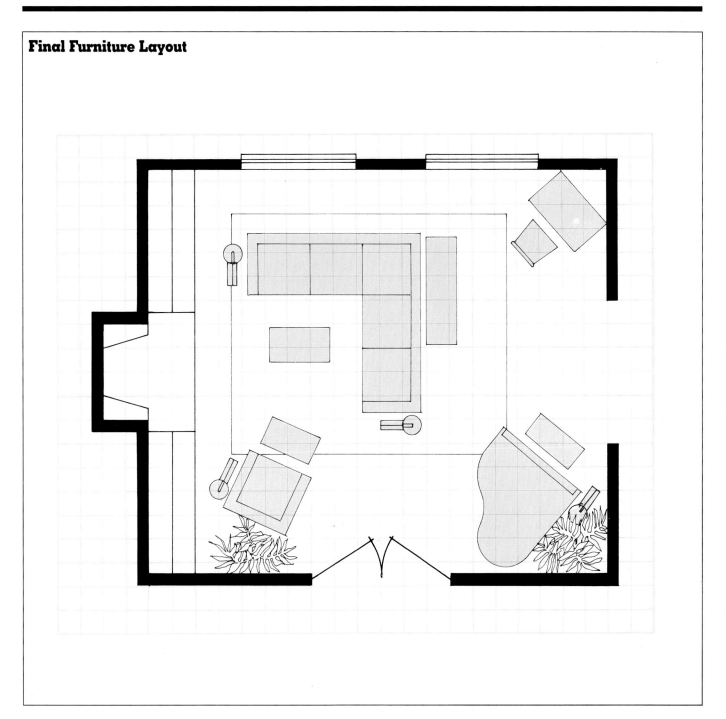

You may discover that, no matter how you've arranged furnishings, something stands in the way of the floor plan you like most. It might be simple to rectify but it might take some structural alterations you hadn't anticipated and are not prepared to implement. If you are baffled at how to make effective changes yourself, this might be a good time to consult with a professional designer to explore your options.

Once you've decided on the final layout, trace the outlines of the relevant furniture shapes on a copy of your original floor plan. If your plan was drawn on a scale of ¼ inch to 1 foot, take this labeled copy to a photocopy shop and have them enlarge the plan fourfold to a scale of 1 inch to 1 foot. Have several copies made and store them in your planning binder for the time being. As you begin to develop the actual design for your room in the next chapter, you'll find the larger floor plan helpful in putting together the colors, fabrics, patterns, and textures that will distinguish your spaces.

Furniture Templates

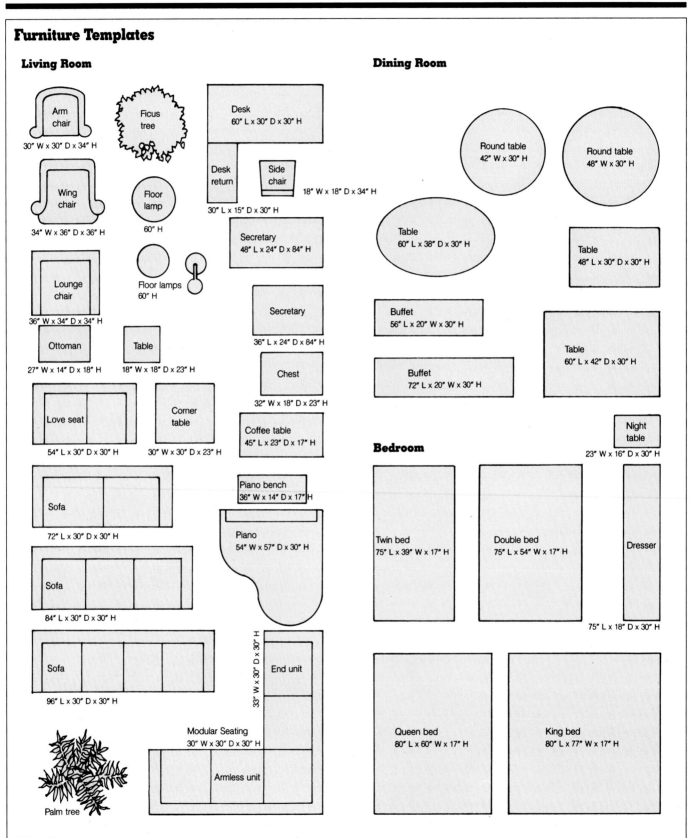

Living Room

Arm chair
30″ W x 30″ D x 34″ H

Ficus tree

Wing chair
34″ W x 36″ D x 36″ H

Floor lamp
60″ H

Lounge chair
36″ W x 34″ D x 34″ H

Floor lamps
60″ H

Ottoman
27″ W x 14″ D x 18″ H

Table
18″ W x 18″ D x 23″ H

Love seat
54″ L x 30″ D x 30″ H

Corner table
30″ W x 30″ D x 23″ H

Sofa
72″ L x 30″ D x 30″ H

Sofa
84″ L x 30″ D x 30″ H

Sofa
96″ L x 30″ D x 30″ H

Palm tree

Modular Seating
30″ W x 30″ D x 30″ H

End unit
33″ W x 30″ D x 30″ H

Armless unit

Desk
60″ L x 30″ D x 30″ H

Desk return
30″ L x 15″ D x 30″ H

Side chair
18″ W x 18″ D x 34″ H

Secretary
48″ L x 24″ D x 84″ H

Secretary
36″ L x 24″ D x 84″ H

Chest
32″ W x 18″ D x 23″ H

Coffee table
45″ L x 23″ D x 17″ H

Piano bench
36″ W x 14″ D x 17″ H

Piano
54″ W x 57″ D x 30″ H

Dining Room

Round table
42″ W x 30″ H

Round table
48″ W x 30″ H

Table
60″ L x 38″ D x 30″ H

Table
48″ L x 30″ D x 30″ H

Buffet
56″ L x 20″ W x 30″ H

Buffet
72″ L x 20″ W x 30″ H

Table
60″ L x 42″ D x 30″ H

Night table
23″ W x 16″ D x 30″ H

Bedroom

Twin bed
75″ L x 39″ W x 17″ H

Double bed
75″ L x 54″ W x 17″ H

Dresser
75″ L x 18″ D x 30″ H

Queen bed
80″ L x 60″ W x 17″ H

King bed
80″ L x 77″ W x 17″ H

¼″ = 1′

Common Clearances

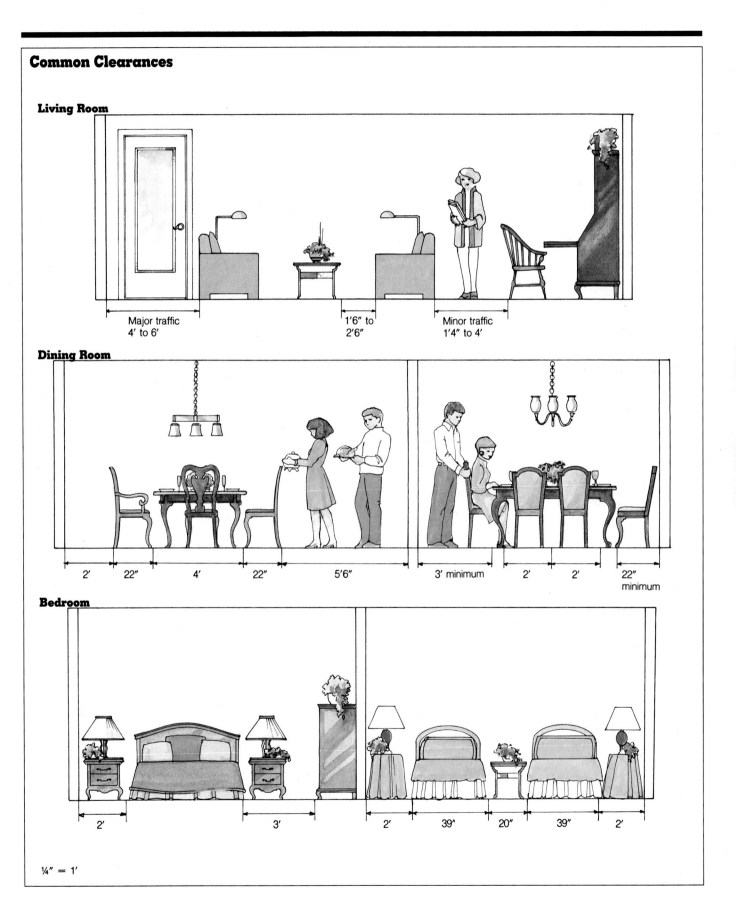

Living Room

Major traffic
4' to 6'

1'6" to
2'6"

Minor traffic
1'4" to 4'

Dining Room

2' 22' 4' 22' 5'6'

3' minimum 2' 2' 22"
minimum

Bedroom

2' 3'

2' 39" 20" 39" 2'

¼" = 1'

PLANNING A COLOR SCHEME

You may already have a color scheme in mind or haven't a clue where to start. This section offers practical guidelines for developing your own color scheme based on the understanding of color you've already gained.

Typical Color Schemes

Although there is no formula for putting colors together in an exact way, over the years a few basic color schemes have evolved. Some suggest that they may have developed as artists experimented with their own color palettes to achieve both harmonious and contrasting effects. Whatever their reason for being, the following schemes can be useful aids in working with color. In particular, they can be helpful in organizing your personal choices into a coherent, harmonious whole that fits your taste and life-style.

Monochromatic

A monochromatic color scheme is built on one hue shown in a number of variations, usually a range that includes one or more tints, a middle value, and some darker shades. Monochromatic schemes may be warm, cool, or largely neutral, and can be enlivened with a little color from another hue for contrast and interest.

A subset of this scheme is the monotone, in which, for instance, the colors employed are primarily tints or shades of one hue—with little variation. Monotones most often appear as a white-on-white scheme, or one based on beige or gray. Keeping monotones from becoming truly monotonous can be offset by adding more texture than usual and by using a variety of patterns within the same tone. The spacious, airy look of a room decorated in pale monotones must be balanced against reality, however: Foot, finger, and paw prints don't mix with those light colors, no matter how much texture or pattern you inject.

Analogous

An analogous color scheme is usually composed of three hues neighboring each other on the color wheel. This scheme appears harmonious to the eye because the hues are closely related and the eye passes smoothly from one to another, regardless of how light or dark the color. Analogous schemes can be put together in a number of ways—a mixture of light, dark, and pure hues in a range of values—and can do much to give a room a unified look along with a strong dose of color.

Complementary

Color schemes that bring together hues opposite each other on the wheel are complementary. The term *complementary*

Cool beige provides a neutral foreground for dramatic views in this monochromatic, contemporary living room.

can be confusing because the word is often used in the context of "going with"—as the side chair complements the sofa. In a complementary scheme, orange and blue at full intensity seldom go together; on the other hand, a dark shade of orange might contrast very nicely with a light tint of blue. Because they combine opposites, complementary schemes offer a balance of warmth and coolness and tend to be livelier and richer in color than either monochromatic or analogous schemes.

A variation of the complementary scheme is the split complementary, formed by combining one hue and the two hues on either side of its complement. An example might be blue, yellow-orange, and red-orange. Warm and cool effects are still possible with a split-complementary solution, but the contrasts are less extreme—especially if you use tints and shades, or tone things down with gray.

Developing Your Own Color Scheme

As a planning exercise, create some quick collages assembled from magazine pictures that appeal to you for their colors, textures, and patterns. Group the pictures into color categories, then decide what groups you like together. Glue them onto cardboard and store them in your planning binder for handy reference.

Warm or Cool Scheme?

Naturally, deciding whether a room will be mainly warm or cool in feeling depends largely on your choice of color, but the decision should also take into consideration the quality of light and orientation to the sun. Natural light from the north has a bluish, cool cast, for example, so if your room looks mainly northward, a scheme built on the cool hues of the color wheel will feel even cooler. If you live in a climate that's warm the year around, you might welcome an interior of cool blues and greens; but if your home is situated in New England, you might think twice about decorating in a very cool scheme.

Opposites

A rule of thumb that works effectively much of the time is to think "opposites"—select hues for the background that fall on the opposite side of the color wheel from the orientation of the room, and accent with hues from the same orientation. For instance, a west- or southwest-facing room receives strong afternoon sun and may be described as warm in its orientation: Selecting blues and greens from the cool side of the wheel for the walls, ceiling, and floor can alleviate the feeling of too much warmth; accenting with small doses of reds and yellows allows the room to retain some of its sunny disposition.

Neutrals

One way to adapt your room to the natural environment without locking yourself into a predetermined warm or cool scheme is to begin with a neutral background, then color furnishings and accessories accordingly. You can help your furnishings flow with the seasons by treating them to a set of slipcovers, covering the warm-hued love seats that help the living room feel so toasty in winter with lighter shades and fabrics as summer approaches. Even changing the colors of an area rug and accessories can work wonders in altering the climate of a room.

Degree

If you'd like a really warm environment, select about 80 percent of your color from the warm side of the wheel, and 20 percent from the cool band. For a mostly warm feeling, choose 60 to 65 percent from the warm hues, 35 to 40 percent from the cool. (Use the same proportions in reverse for a cool environment.) Generally speaking, dividing warm and cool hues into an exact 50/50 distribution is confusing to the eye because it has difficulty responding to how the room feels.

Light or Dark Scheme?

The next step is to determine whether the values of the color families you plan to use will be mainly dark or light—shades or tints—or fall somewhere in the middle range. Again, orientation to natural light plays a role, as does the intended function of the room and the nature of your life-style. If the laundry room is extragloomy because, let's say, a tall evergreen blocks out the sun, yet you don't want to use too many light values because the area also serves as the mudroom and pet-feeding area, you might opt for middle or slightly darker values for the floor and lower cabinetry and lighter values for the upper walls and ceiling. Or you can choose a mostly dark scheme to disguise the dirt, and compensate for the lack of daylight with well-planned artificial lighting.

Degree

Figuring out the amount of dark, light, and middle values can be approached in the same way you determined the degree of warmth and coolness. For a predominately dark (or light) environment, think in terms of an 80 percent/20 percent split; for a moderately dark (or light) room, think 60 percent/40 percent.

Gradations

Regardless of how you distribute light and dark in your room, however, it's important to include gradations, or steps, between the lightest and darkest values to avoid too much contrast.

In a room setting, choosing five steps between the lightest and darkest values works effectively, especially when you vary the intensities of color as well. These gradations can be widely spread across the value scale or they may be grouped tightly, as when you seek to achieve a monotone. When a scheme doesn't have increments of color between the extremes—or enough of them—the room may seem to lack unity, balance, and rhythm. In addition, if most of the values fall at one end of the scale, the eye will go to the exception at the other end and linger there. That's fine if you wish to emphasize an accent or a particular piece of furniture, but it's a disadvantage if your goal is to give equal weight to the various elements of the room.

Making a Sample Board

Now that you've thought through the degree of warm and cool, and the distribution of light and dark, you're ready to select the actual colors for your color scheme. Bear in mind, though, that finalizing your scheme is only one phase of developing the overall room design—albeit an important one—and should proceed in conjunction with selecting materials for floor, ceiling, walls, windows, and furnishings. The following exercises that describe how to make sample boards will help you narrow down what really works in terms of color, pattern, and texture before you do any buying at all.

There is no prescribed way to build a sample board, but the accompanying photograph demonstrates one method that works well. The board presents colors and materials in their approximate distributions and arranged in about the same order as you'd expect to see them in a room: the flooring material positioned across the bottom; wall and window treatments, accents, and furnishing fabrics represented in the center; and ceiling color and finish at the top. Assembling the board in this way offers the flexibility to change samples that don't seem to suit your color scheme.

Supplies

Have all your materials on hand before you begin. Art supplies should consist of photocopies of your original floor plans, elevations, and the final furniture layout and its corresponding elevations (at least several copies of each); several 11- by 16-inch cardboard sheets; a set of colored pencils or a box of crayons (at least 64 colors); and glue. For color, pattern, and texture samples, use paint chips, colored paper, photographs, wrapping paper, wallpaper, fabrics, bits of carpet, and so on.

Set Down Color

Gather together the flat paper swatches of all the solid colors you plan to incorporate. Be sure to include swatches that show steps of color from subtle to bright, as well as gradations in value. Distribute the colors proportionally as you intend to use them in your room, remembering that walls typically occupy two thirds of a space, whereas accents account for a much smaller area. You may have to cut some swatches smaller, and tape together others of the same color to achieve the right distribution. Arrange the papers on a piece of cardboard (8 by 11 inches or larger) so that none of the cardboard shows, and glue them in place. You can arrange them in random order to provide an overall sense of color distribution; or you can line up the papers so that the floor color occupies the bottom, the ceiling the top, and the wall and furnishing colors the areas in between.

Deciding Texture and Pattern

Set aside the color board and give some thought to texture, actual and visual, and where you'd like to use it in the room—without assigning a particular color. Will texture appear on the floor, on the fireplace surround, in furnishings, in the plants? Choose gradations in texture (five is a good number here, too), from absolutely flat and smooth, like glass, to rough and nubby, like a basket or a woven wall hanging. Strong texture on the floor will "ground" it, so if you don't want to emphasize that surface, keep the texture subtle and focus on something else. Follow the same process with pattern, again concentrating on where you want to use pattern, and how much, rather than on the exact colors. You can intermix stripes, plaids, florals, abstracts, and so forth, as long as they appear visually pleasing and are appropriate to the scale of the furnishings and the room.

Put Color, Texture, and Pattern in Place

Pull out the copies of the original floor plan and elevations. Color in the floors and walls on the basic room plan as closely as you can according to your paper swatches. (It's unlikely that you'll be able to duplicate colors exactly.) Then, where appropriate, over the colors draw in some of the textures and patterns you have in mind for the background. Don't worry about being too precise; this is just an exercise. Once you've arrived at a distribution that seems right, repeat the same exercise on a copy of the final layout and its elevations, assigning color, pattern, and texture to specific items such as furnishings, lamps, and window coverings.

You may find that what seemed desirable in concept looks only fair on the floor plan, or that the room appears to need more contrast to keep it from being bland, or that the cabbage-sized floral you had imagined for the sofa is wrong for the scale of the room. You may decide to do the exercise all over again on fresh copies using a slightly different set of hues, or the same ones in different proportions. Coloring in your floor plans won't give you an accurate color picture, but it will help you assess—and reassess—your intended scheme.

Add Actual Samples

Now, to bring the color scheme closer to life, incorporate real fabrics, paints, wallcoverings, and floor coverings onto a sample board. If you've already collected more samples than you can possibly use, you might like to develop two boards, variations of the same overall scheme; later, you can refine them into your final selections. If you're still gathering materials, take along your colored floor plans and the paper collage to help choose the samples that best fit your scheme.

In making the board, again lay out the sample materials in the approximate distribution you'd find in your room without letting the cardboard show through. Ideally, of course, you would put samples in their exact proportions, but that's not always a practical solution. Paint chips representing the actual expanse of walls might take up most of the board, for instance, and the scrap of fabric representing a chair ends up so small as to be visually lost.

Once you've tailored the board to your satisfaction, it's time to try out the same scheme on a bigger scale. Using your colored plans and sample boards as guides, go back to the dealers who supplied the samples in the first place. Beg, borrow, or buy, if necessary, large

enough samples to make some impact in a full-sized room: a can of paint to try out on the walls (or on a large piece of cardboard to lean against a wall); flooring samples measuring at least 18 by 24 inches (the bigger, the better); bolts of your first-choice fabrics (if borrowing

isn't possible, and the fabric is not too expensive, buy a yard of each); long samples of wall-covering (many stores lend out 6- or 8-foot strips).

Keep track of the way the materials look and feel over a period of several days; move them around the room to observe how changes in natural and artificial light affect their color and mood, then evaluate them again in terms of your living patterns. Sample boards are valuable aids, but represent only a part of the picture. Once you've seen the bigger samples in place, you may need to rethink some of the materials and readjust your proposed color scheme. But that's part of the challenge, and fun, of developing a decorating style that serves function, life-style, and personal taste—and will please you for a long time to come.

A potential color scheme comes to life on this sample board and floor plan.

DEVELOPING YOUR DESIGN

With the all-important process of planning complete, including selection of a color scheme, you can turn your attention to developing your actual design. This chapter will help you examine different aspects of your room one by one, offer tips for evaluating and buying materials, and make suggestions for ways to put your design into action with an eye to function and life-style. The first portion of this chapter discusses many materials and finishes available for the surfaces of your room—floor, ceiling, walls, and windows—and will help you select them. Subsequent sections discuss furnishings (with an emphasis on matching materials and looks with needs, life-style, and budget), lighting, and the finishing touches that come with accessories.

An heirloom painted leather screen sets the color scheme of this vibrant living room. The formality of the paneled marble fireplace and seating arrangement is offset by country touches—folk art, distressed woods, rug-covered plank flooring, and whimsical accessories.

FLOOR COVERINGS

Floor covering is a key element in establishing the character and aesthetics of a space because it anchors a room both physically and visually. The floor takes more of a beating than any other surface, so materials must be chosen with an eye to wearability and maintenance as well as appearance.

Determining the Function

Whether you settle on a hard flooring such as marble, tile, or wood, choose a material that is soft underfoot, or combine the two within the same space, begin your homework by determining your practical needs and examining your options.

Since new flooring is comparatively costly, and will probably be left in place at least for several years, it makes sense to analyze the room in which it will be used and once again review your family life-style. Where will the flooring be used and who will use it? What kinds of activities will take place and how often? Heavy foot traffic or light? Potential for food spills, paw prints? Lots of sunshine or moisture? Does the room exit to the outdoors? Is the priority comfort, low maintenance, insulation against noise and climate? What's the condition of the existing flooring? Could it be recycled, refinished, redyed? What about the subfloor? How much have you budgeted to spend?

Selecting what's most appropriate for the situation can be challenging. If, for instance, you're concentrating on one room at the moment, but you'd eventually like to use the same material throughout the living areas to unify the spaces, you might have to invest the time and expense in having the flooring installed all at once to guarantee that colors, grain, and finish match up room to room. On the other hand, if the room in question has a floor you can live with a little bit longer, you might give it a temporary cover-up with a painted design, an area rug you can reuse in the same space, or an inexpensive all-purpose jute or sisal covering extending wall to wall.

Once you have a handle on the practical requirements, you'll find that narrowing the range of possibilities becomes an easier task. Then you can explore the aesthetics of the various alternatives to discover which best suits your personal style and the decorating look you're after. Is this a room where you intend to make the floor a focal point or just part of the background? Is the mood to be formal, semiformal, or casual? How do you wish to integrate the flooring into your color scheme? Happily, there's a tremendous variety in the hard and soft floor coverings available today. The following descriptions of the major categories of flooring will give you

Don't be locked into one type of floor covering when your needs might be better met by several. Easy-care ceramic tile is a good choice for an entry. A carpeted stairway cushions noise and is easy underfoot.

some basic information to help guide you through the selection process.

Masonry

The most durable of flooring materials, masonry includes stone, such as marble, granite, and slate; ceramic and quarry tile; brick; and concrete. Masonry is intended to last for years, and on the average is more expensive than wood, resilient flooring, or carpet. Its reputation for durability and longevity is offset by an inherent hardness that can be problematic: Masonry is subject to chipping and cracking; it's jarring to walk on and tiring to stand on for more than a short time; and it can be noisy and cold to the touch. Masonry is also heavy—a 1-foot square of 1-inch-thick slate can weigh 15 to 20 pounds—and typically requires installation by a professional.

Marble and Granite

Especially when their surfaces are polished to highlight veining, colors, and patterns, marble and granite are the most elegant and formal members of the stone family. They are also the most expensive. Granite is harder and stronger than marble, more concentrated, and extremely durable. On average it's about double the cost of marble and three to four times more than slate. Usually sold in 6- by 12-inch slabs, granite is also available in sheets of varying thicknesses for use on surfaces such as kitchen countertops. All stone is slippery when wet, so if you're considering granite as a flooring

material, select a variety with a textured, or "flamed" surface. A few coats of a stone sealer will keep a granite floor looking its best.

Quickly recognized for its delicate veining and range of color, marble is usually sold in 12- by 12-inch sheets. It is an extremely porous material and should always be well-sealed with a marble filler-sealant or several coats of wax, especially in areas where spills occur or water collects. If you plan to use marble as the bathroom flooring, it is recommended that sheets be cut down to 6-inch squares; the smaller size and extra grout give texture underfoot and provide a measure of safety against slipping.

Slate

As a flooring material slate has been held in high regard for years: it is reasonably priced, adapts to both formal and casual decorating schemes, and requires minimal upkeep. Slate is resistant to most stains but it does absorb oil, so sealing is recommended. In addition, a coat of wax will mask scuffs in heavy traffic areas.

If you'd like to incorporate marble, granite, or slate into your flooring plans, but your budget won't permit purchasing enough for a large expanse, use it sparingly—only in the guest bath, for example, or in combination with hardwood as the focal point of the front hall.

Ceramic Tile

Unquestionably one of the most versatile flooring options available to the homeowner,

ceramic tile is also one of the easiest to maintain. A browse through a well-stocked tile store will reveal a color wheel of hues, sizes ranging from 1-inch-square mosaics to 12- by 12-inch sheets, glazed and unglazed finishes, and a variety of decorative themes and motifs. Because there are literally hundreds of ways to combine tiles, you can create floor designs to suit virtually any color scheme or decorating style—and do so on a limited budget. You can create patterns and borders, design a tile "area rug," section off a part of a room as a tile-floor conservatory to hold plants. You can even have the elegant effect of marble or granite with look-alike tiles—at a third of the cost of the stone originals.

Ceramic tile is fashioned from fire-hardened clay and is usually glazed with a smooth gloss or matte finish that makes the surface highly resistant to stains, water damage, and burns. A close cousin to ceramic tile is porcelain tile, which is fired at a higher temperature and is therefore stronger; porcelain tile is typically used in areas with a lot of foot traffic or where durability is an issue. Unglazed tile is also fire hardened, but the color usually runs throughout the tile and the surface carries a matte finish with a slight texture that makes the tile less slippery than glazed tile when wet.

Quarry tile is produced from kiln-fired natural clay, usually unglazed or lightly glazed, and is distinguished by its natural clay coloration—typically terracotta or brown tones, but sometimes tending toward rose, blue,

or gray. Quarry tile is manufactured in a variety of shapes and sizes, from rectangles to hexagons to interlocking keyhole shapes. Its durability makes it an excellent choice for heavy-traffic areas and indoor-outdoor rooms, and its irregular surface offers protection against slipping. Most quarry tile is stain resistant, but some varieties—Mexican pavers, for instance—require sealing to keep them looking their best.

Brick and Concrete

Though brick and concrete constitute flooring in some homes, they are far less common than tile or stone. A brick floor can add visual charm to a rustic country kitchen, but it is hard underfoot and uncomfortably rough unless covered with several coats of wax. Left unwaxed, brick still needs a sealer to protect it against scratches, grease, and stains—unless you install a brick veneer that's been high-fired against cracking and presealed against stains. Like quarry tile, brick can be a good material for indoor-outdoor areas.

If you've ever walked barefoot across a concrete garage floor, you already know that as a material it is cold and hard. But if you're turning an area with a concrete floor into, let's say, a recreation room, you can usually cover the concrete with any of several other materials. Its smooth, durable surface makes a fine base for stone and tile, and with proper preparation it will accept a covering such as wood, resilient flooring, or carpet.

Wood

Among flooring materials, wood remains a traditional favorite—perhaps because of its association with nature or because it integrates well with virtually any style of furniture and any decorating look. Wood flooring is highly durable and can last nearly as long as stone. Its physical structure gives its surface a resiliency that's less tiring to stand on than masonry, less likely to result in breakage when things fall, and far quieter. Moreover, thanks to modern stains and sealers, wood flooring is a renewable resource in the home—easier than ever to refinish or decorate with creative surface treatments.

Within the family of woods suitable for flooring are some hardwoods, harvested from leaf-bearing trees such as maple, oak, walnut, and birch, and some softwoods, cut from a variety of conifers, such as pine, fir, cedar, and redwood. Oak is the most common hardwood flooring in today's homes, because of its proven durability and ready acceptance of stain, but softer woods are sometimes used, especially if the desired effect is the imperfect look of worn floorboards.

Availability

Typically, wood flooring is available in three types: strips—long, narrow boards fitted together side by side; planks—wider boards (8 to 12 inches) that are also installed side by side but in a random pattern; and predesigned squares or blocks, which may resemble a section of strip or plank floor or be arranged in a parquet pattern. Parquet squares are usually fashioned from a mosaic of hardwood veneers—oak, walnut, and mahogany—fitted together in decorative patterns and glued onto a softwood base.

Finishes

Most strip and plank flooring comes unfinished, so after installation you can finish it to suit your decorating needs—stain it all one shade, or create your own patterns by making a lighter or darker border, inserting a sunburst in the center, or devising a checkerboard pattern. You can also purchase wood flooring that's been prefinished in a variety of shades—including pastels—and impregnated at the factory with a tough polyurethane sealer. One process, called end-graining, lends wood flooring a striped, striated appearance by

A warm, polished hardwood floor is part of a country look.

If your floor is in poor condition, a stenciled, painted pattern will give it new life.

New Looks With Paint for Old Wood Floors

Refurbishing a worn wood floor can be done in several ways. You can sand it down and refinish it with a new stain or lighten it with bleach. Alternatively, you can create a host of special effects with paint. Easy to work with, and eminently affordable, paint is especially good for floors that aren't easily refinished by conventional means. Moreover, a painted floor is an ideal interim solution to a problem surface that you may wish to replace altogether with new flooring later on when the budget allows.

Regardless of the paint technique you choose—washing (or pickling), stenciling, spattering, or marbleizing—here are a few suggestions to help the process go smoothly. There are professionals who specialize in these techniques—get references from a local interior designer, flooring dealer, or paint company—or you may try your own artistic hand with guidance from a book such as Ortho's *Floors & Floor Coverings*.

For any kind of overall floor design, it is a good idea to make a preliminary drawing to help you visualize the result. You might want to make photocopies of the grid paper and completed floor plan in your planning binder to be sure that the size and shape of your design will suit the proportions of the room and your intended placement of furnishings. Try out several different designs, keeping in mind that an overall pattern, such as a large-scale checkerboard, will look quite different when it is transferred to the floor.

Washing, or Pickling

To lighten a floor with paint rather than bleach, apply a paint tint of your choice with a brush or a roller, then wipe it off before it starts to dry. The wiping motion encourages the paint to seep into the cracks and knots of the wood, creating variations in color and texture in softwood, and lightening hardwood, such as oak, in a more uniform way.

Stenciling

You can add pattern to a floor with stenciling, whether as a border, a painted-on area rug or floor cloth, or a light motif that simply meanders across the surface. Stenciling requires careful planning to keep colors and proportions compatible with the overall floor area and the feeling of the room. You can purchase precut stencils from an art-supply store; copy a theme from a wallcovering or fabric that you intend to use in the room; select a geometric pattern that's fairly easy to lay out, such as checkerboard or diamond shapes; or create your own artistic design. If your present floor is in fairly good condition, you may want to limit the design to a border or keep it small and simple.

Spattering

Unlike stenciling, spattering is an informal technique that requires minimal planning, and can even become a family project. Usually, the floor receives a base coat of paint, then the spattering is applied by manipulating the bristles of the paint brush—striking the handle with a stick, flicking the wrist, or whatever works best to achieve the desired effect. The process can be messy, so you might want to protect windows and walls with plastic drop cloths or old sheets. Spattering is a good cover-up for heavy-traffic areas because its random pattern helps mask scuffs, scrapes, and dirt.

Marbleizing

As the name suggests, marbleizing attempts to imitate the colors and veining of marble (or other stone). Achieving a true marble look on a painted floor takes patience and practice, but when mastered can transform the ordinary into the elegant. It helps to have a practice session, referring to a photograph or an actual piece of marble to make the veining look believable. When you perform the actual painting process, complete one section at a time, as if you were installing marble sheets one by one.

---

sandwiching thin layers of differently stained woods on a diagonal, gluing them to a base, and slicing them into strips. Many predesigned and parquet squares are available with adhesive backings, so you can install them like tile, following your own design instincts or using the manufacturer's suggestions.

All wood needs a finish of some sort. If you're planning to install an unfinished variety, you'll need to stain and seal—at least seal—the surface. You might prefer to apply a penetrating sealer, let it dry, and then protect it with several coats of good-quality wax. Or you may choose to seal the surface with a polyurethane finish, which has proven to be more durable and water-resistant than conventional varnish, and

easy to maintain on a day-to-day basis. Polyurethane tends to darken the surface, however, so if you plan to apply it over a paint or stain base, remember to adjust colors accordingly.

There are advantages to each method of finishing. The combination of penetrating sealer and wax can give the floor a rich glow that's visually satisfying. When properly waxed, the surface can be nearly as easy to maintain as one coated with polyurethane; and when it needs refurbishing, the wax may be removed and reapplied without harming the sealer beneath. Polyurethane offers a finish that's unbeatable for high-traffic areas; but when it has worn off (that can be as soon as a year), the entire floor requires retreating—resanding and a reapplication of polyurethane.

Resilient Flooring

Resilient floor coverings are a popular compromise between the hardness of stone and tile and the softness of carpet. Like wood, resilient flooring is comfortable underfoot and suits many decorating needs and moods. It is lightweight, easy to maintain, and can cover stain-prone areas not suited for fine hardwoods or carpet. Moreover, resilient flooring is reasonably priced and available in countless colors and patterns, including those that mimic stone, wood, and hand-painted tile. It even lends itself to decorative treatments in the form of borders, inlays, and custom patterns, from geometrics and stripes to abstract designs.

Vinyl

Topping the list of resilient flooring in today's homes is vinyl, a completely synthetic material. It may be solid, which means that at least 60 percent of the weight of its binder comes from strong, resilient, long-lasting vinyl resins, or composition, made up of a lesser amount of vinyl resins plus fillers. In addition, vinyl flooring may be inlaid or printed. The colors and designs seen on the surface of inlaid vinyl extend through the material to the backing in a series of heat-fused layers, producing a long-wearing surface. Printed vinyls are sometimes called rotovinyls because colors and patterns are printed on the surface layer through a rotogravure process; the vinyl picture is mounted on a cushiony material and then attached to the backing. Rotovinyls are less costly than inlaid varieties, but the patterns can wear off with time and disappear with a gouge or a chip.

Vinyl flooring may be purchased in sheets cut from 6-, 12-, or 15-foot rolls, or in tiles, usually measuring 12 by 12 inches but as large as 36 by 36 inches. Tiles and sheeting are both available in so many textures, colors, and patterns that opting for one or the other can be decided by your lifestyle, budget, and decorating plans rather than availability.

Vinyl sheeting is becoming increasingly popular with homeowners because it's comparatively easy to care for. Because fewer seams are possible with 12- and 15-foot widths, there are fewer places to collect dirt particles and potentially become unglued. Surfaces are protected with glass-smooth finishes that wipe clean quickly and demand more thorough attention only once in a while.

Vinyl tile offers tremendous potential if you want to create a geometric design on your floor, and it is a good choice if you wish to attain the effect of marble or quarry tile without the expense. Solid vinyl tile—far more durable than composition

Resilient floor coverings make it easy to create custom decorative treatments because they are available in many patterns and colors.

Structural Details

If you'd like to create the impression of a structural change without touching the structure, you can add false beams to your present ceiling or visually drop a portion of it by suspending a false ceiling over part of the room. If the idea of a beamed ceiling fits into your plans, you can purchase hollow U-shaped wood beams that offer a massive look without the weight, then stain them to match woodwork, built-in cabinetry, and flooring. If your goal is a painted ceiling with some architectural interest, you might investigate beams and moldings fashioned from superlight urethane that accepts paint without sanding and priming. Even an ordinary 8-foot ceiling can be made more interesting with coved molding that unites ceiling and walls in a graceful curve.

Dropping a portion of the ceiling even a few inches around the perimeter of a room can make the central area seem higher than it really is; by the same token, lowering the ceiling over, let's say, the dining area of a multiuse room can serve to separate it visually and psychologically from the rest of the space. A suspended ceiling may be fashioned from a variety of materials—from wood lattice to wallboard to fabric-covered panels. When a false ceiling conceals lighting that bounces off the structural ceiling and adjacent walls, the mood of the entire room can be altered.

Lighting, in fact, can do more to give life to a ceiling than you might imagine. Track lighting is one of the easiest types to install and is available in fixtures that vary greatly in shape, size, type of lamp, and finish. The section on lighting in this chapter (see page 84) presents suggestions for illuminating ceilings to show them at their best.

The ceiling is definitely part of the decorating scheme if covered with reflective tiles. Their slick surface is in keeping with the look of this contemporary interior.

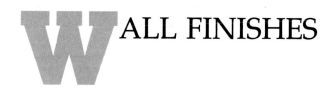

WALL FINISHES

When you consider just how much surface of a room is devoted to walls, knowing exactly what you want your walls to do and which treatment or material is the best choice becomes an important decorating decision.

Treatments

From cave paintings to medieval tapestries to the full range of modern-day wallcoverings, the decoration of walls has been a dominant factor in shaping the character of rooms. Wall treatments can play down the defects of a room while drawing attention to its assets; create visual beauty and physical warmth; offer textures and patterns that lend surface appeal; counterbalance a focal-point floor; make spaces seem larger or smaller; even divert attention from a modest or sparse grouping of furnishings.

At this stage of your decorating plan, you probably know whether you wish the colors of your room to feel mainly warm or cool, or look mostly light or dark. You may even have begun the process of developing your actual decorating scheme. Regardless of the colors you select, however, you can broaden the horizons of your room greatly by investigating a number of potential wall finishes, including some that go beyond the familiar paint-and-paper solutions.

Paint

An all-time favorite wall treatment, paint is easy to apply, economically priced, and available in a wide range of hues, tints, and shades. The great transformer of ceilings and walls alike, paint can do wonders to change the feeling and appearance of a space. A boxy room will appear longer when end walls are painted a lighter color than the others, shorter when given a darker shade; the room can look larger altogether when all the surfaces are painted the same light tint. Warm-hued paints decrease the apparent size of a room, as do high-intensity colors, because they make the walls seem to advance toward you. Paints that are cool in hue and light in value do just the opposite, making the walls appear to recede. A matte paint finish in a sunny room will soften the intensity of the light, whereas a high-gloss finish will create uncomfortable glare. On the other hand, a dark high-gloss paint will reflect both natural and artificial light and may be the ideal finish for a dim room.

Special Finishes

Single-color paints can offer a textured look when applied over a stucco or plaster finish or when sand is mixed in with the paint itself. Flat surfaces can become infinitely more interesting visually when they are manipulated with special paint effects. These decorative finishes—some of them surprisingly easy to achieve—can also hide unsightly blemishes, uneven surfaces, and awkward angles in both ceilings and walls. Furthermore, they can bring both style and romance to otherwise ordinary settings through artistic touches that can be as simple as a faux, or false, finish reminiscent of drifting clouds or silk brocade, or as detailed as a mural of the rolling countryside or a trompe l'oeil finish that tricks the eye into seeing a true-to-life picture on the wall.

Painted Decorative Effects

Painting a mural, or even a modest trompe l'oeil scene, may be more complicated than your own artistic skills can handle, so if you're interested in pursuing that particular effect you'll probably want to contact someone who specializes in painted effects. But there are a number of decorative finishes that are not difficult to attain with a little practice. They use standard paints and glazes and easy-to-find tools that may be as close as your utility closet. Classes are available where you can learn how to apply them yourself. Or, budget permitting, you can hire a specialist to create them for you.

Painted trim and borders add visual excitement to plain walls.

Glazing is simply the application of a transparent film over an opaque base to add richness and depth to a wall. *Dragging* and *combing* add texture to a glazed surface. In the first method, a dry wide paintbrush, wire brush, or whisk broom is pulled across or down the wet glaze, for an irregular striated or striped effect. The second technique results in a similar look—though the stripes are more prominent—by scoring the wet glaze with the edge of a piece of corrugated cardboard, a squeegie, or a windshield wiper blade with teeth cut into the rubber, or even an old dustpan with grooves notched into its rubber edge. Another way to alter the surface is by *stippling*—a more time-consuming process that

requires dabbing the tips of a dry brush against the wet glaze. It results in an interesting dappled, mottled, orange-peel texture.

Ragging produces soft effects suggestive of fabric. Materials such as burlap, gauze, cheesecloth, or old sheets or towels each lend a slightly different appearance to the wall surface. If the rag is crumpled before it is dipped into the glaze and then is used like a roller, the surface will resemble crushed velvet; if the rag is bunched up and the glaze is then blotted on, the surface will look more like clouds; if several rags are bundled up and each used to apply the glaze in changing directions, the surface will resemble damask or brocade. Alternatively, the glaze can be

first brushed on the wall, then covered with a second layer that is rolled on with a tightly wadded or twisted dry rag to create a distressed appearance.

Sponging is one of the easiest techniques and can produce delicate, even fanciful, decorative effects. There are two ways to execute the finish: Using a natural sea sponge, the glaze is applied onto the base coat of paint; or, a layer of glaze is brushed over the base and then dabbed off with the sponge. One layer of sponging gives a light, variegated effect; several layers of a sponged-on tinted glaze creates an almost iridescent, pearl-like surface.

Faux marble finishes are a little trickier to accomplish because it's more difficult to

imitate a real material than to create imaginative effects. First, a base coat is applied that approximates the background color of a particular type of marble. A white or tinted glaze is used for the marble effect over a dark base; for a light undercoat, a slightly darker glaze and an even darker shade for veining is necessary. To create a variegated look, a bunched-up or crumpled soft rag is dipped in the glaze and dabbed lightly on the walls, while rubbing slightly to blur any sharp edges; the finish is then left to dry. The process is repeated with sponging techniques. Veins are applied with a fine-tip artist's brush that's been dipped in glaze, then smudged slightly with the corner of a rag or a goose feather.

A painted faux finish textures the walls of this formal library.

An old-fashioned bathroom is renewed with paint.

Coverings

Wallcoverings usually offer more emphasis and visual texture than paint—certainly more pattern, if you wish it. They can divert the eye from noticing structural flaws, hide surface imperfections, and create interest in a room that has none architecturally. They can be very effective in making rooms with few furnishings seem full. Wallcoverings do belong in the background of rooms, however, and should generally be selected to blend with and unify the spaces rather than dominate them.

Wallpaper

Choosing wallpaper can be a mind-boggling task if you go through sample books page by page. Papers can be textured in any of a number of ways or be perfectly smooth. They can be patterned with florals, geometrics, animal motifs, and ethnic themes, or be of such a subtle design that the surface more closely resembles paint. Their scale can be large, medium, small, or mini. They can be protected with a vinyl coating for cleaning ease, and backed with fabric for durability. Some come with a prepasted backing for easy hanging. Most wallpapers are fabricated entirely by machine, but some are made by a hand printing and painting process. Many are designed to coordinate with other papers and companion fabrics; some even have matching tiles. In short, there are so many options available that it will simplify your decision-making if you eliminate the patterns, scales, themes, and colors that won't work for your room and focus on only those wallpaper books that match your needs.

Not all of the coverings commonly dubbed wallpaper are true papers, however. Grass cloth, for instance, is composed of natural fibers attached to a paper backing; fabrics such as linen and silk also come backed with paper. Metallics are largely foils.

Fabrics

Some fabrics make excellent wallcoverings; in bygone days they were the primary surface cover to add warmth and decoration. Almost any fabric can be tacked or stapled directly onto a wall or ceiling; if you don't want to mar the surface, you can staple the fabric to a wood frame that's been secured to the wall in a few places. Tight, straight weaves tend to hold their shape best, and the thicker the material, the better it will hide flawed walls. A loose-weave cloth such as burlap requires a little more attention in the hanging process to keep it from being stretched or pulled out of shape. Lightweight and sheer fabrics look better when they are gathered slightly, or shirred, before stapling; their soft folds lend a luxurious air to a room and can conceal a host of wall problems, such as unwanted textures, difficult-to-repair cracks, or an old wallcovering that can't be removed without a great deal of effort.

Wood

Of course, there are more ways to cover a wall than with paint or paper—wood, for instance. Wood paneling is a warm, natural addition to a room; and although it is more expensive than paint and most papers on a foot-by-foot basis, wood paneling is easy to care for, simple to install, and will last for years. Most paneling is available in a wide variety of wood finishes and is sold in 4- by 8-foot sheets composed of a thin

Wallpaper can camouflage structural problems such as an angled ceiling, and can make a large space appear more intimate.

veneer of hardwood atop a plywood or processed-wood base. The hardwood surface is normally prefinished at the factory to seal the wood and enhance the finish.

If you don't wish to invest in paneling an entire room, but like the idea of a paneled wall in, let's say, the utility room or your thirteen-year-old son's bedroom, you can consider less expensive plywood paneling that uses a vinyl or paper overlay to simulate a wood grain. Such panels are only moderately durable and some are more realistic looking than others, but if you're planning to use them sparingly or replace them with something else in a few years, they can be a smart choice. Another possibility is plywood paneling with a

rough-sawn finish—less costly than prefinished panels and distinctly rustic in appearance.

Sometimes a simple wood lattice makes an effective wallcovering: Painted a color that is similar to the wall underneath, it can add depth and texture to the surface; left in its natural state, or painted in a contrasting color, it can create a trellislike pattern that gives a sense of perspective to the space. Or you can make your own wall designs with solid boards or strips laid on the diagonal or in patterns. The variations in texture can set up understated but definite rhythms that please the eye.

Mirrors

Among wallcoverings, mirrors are unique in their ability to enlarge a space visually while

creating bright patterns of reflected light. Depending on their location on a wall, they can double—or even triple—the apparent size of a space. An especially welcome addition to a small, dim room, a mirrored wall can make the wall itself seem to disappear and the adjacent spaces appear to flow right through the mirror and beyond. Strips of mirror on either side of a fireplace may give the impression of looking into another room; when placed on either side of a door and positioned to reflect a window view, the strips resemble glass sidelights offering glimpses of the outdoors. Used in a narrow band around the perimeter of a room just below the ceiling,

mirrors can help a room look both wider and taller by bouncing natural and artificial light onto ceiling and upper walls. Installed like a baseboard close to the floor, mirrors will visually increase the floor area in all directions, and are especially effective space expanders when they reflect a flooring material that stretches wall to wall.

Mirror tiles are less expensive than plate mirror and are easy to install. Shiny, pressed-metal ceiling tiles are also reasonably priced and can behave somewhat like mirrors when placed on the wall, expanding space and bouncing light around; their heavily textured surfaces distort the images they reflect, creating unusual patterns and giving surfaces the appearance of sculpture.

Wood paneling doesn't always mean stuffy and formal. Here, wide planks make a sophisticated yet low-key backdrop for contemporary furnishings.

Mirrors expand small spaces and open up otherwise static walls.

WINDOW TREATMENTS

Of all the architectural elements in your home, windows have a unique position: they serve as the visual link with the outside world and the primary source of natural light. The key to selecting the right covering lies in knowing how you want your windows to function and how well the treatment will adapt to your family life-style.

Which Type?

If your windows reveal a pleasing view, you may wish to employ a minimal covering—possibly nothing at all. On the other hand, if you're concerned with privacy, or insulation against heat or cold, or blocking an unpleasant view, then finding the balance between covering the window and still letting in light can become a decorating challenge.

There are many alternatives in window treatments. The challenge is choosing the right one for your needs. Begin with function: Do you want to frame a good view or hide a bad one? Is privacy a motivating factor? Too much sunlight, or too many drafts? Do you want a covering that opens wide in the daytime and closes tightly at night? Is noise from the street a factor? Or will the treatment be mainly decorative, to enhance a theme or mood?

Now quiz yourself on your life-style. Maintenance is a good place to start. If you want most of the window to show, will you be able to keep the expanse of glass clean? On kitchen windows, where grease can collect, will the material be easy to wash or have professionally cleaned? Huge folds of fabric, billowy shades, and shirred sheers all gather cobwebs and dust. Do you have the patience to vacuum pleats and folds one by one? And, whereas you don't usually have to worry about wear and tear on windows as you do on floors, sun and humidity can deteriorate the covering. And

what about expense? Window coverings, like so much else that goes into your home, can range from the absolutely affordable—rice paper shades and plain cotton curtains, for instance—to costly custom treatments that employ only the finest materials and workmanship.

Once you have evaluated how you want your windows to fit your life-style, you can better decide which treatment matches the style of your home and your decorating scheme.

The window in this young man's room is relatively small and without architectural interest. With an overscale drapery treatment, the window achieves some importance and becomes a focal point.

Fabric Coverings

As window dressings, curtains and draperies are probably the most versatile coverings, because they can be adapted to virtually every window shape and size and fashioned into the simplest of styles, or the most elaborate. The secret to their versatility is simple: fabric. The ability of fabric to flow, drape, soften sharp angles and hard textures, and be manipulated into a variety of forms makes it an ideal solution for even the most problematic window. And fabric comes in a wide array of patterns, colors, textures, and fibers. Beyond curtains and draperies, fabric finds its way into shades and specialty window treatments, such as valances and swags (see the brief glossary of window terms on page 69).

Curtains and Draperies

Though the lines separating the two coverings are somewhat blurred, curtains typically refer to layers of lightweight fabric hanging from rods to the sill or below, and draperies are panels of medium- to heavyweight fabric that also hang vertically, usually to the floor. Because curtains are frequently relatively sheer, they permit filtered light (and views) and are easily paired with blinds or roller shades for privacy. Draperies are often teamed with curtains when the decorating mood is formal or the theme traditional, but they are equally appropriate hanging alone. When curtain or drapery fabric is stretched across the top of a window in a graceful swag to join the matching panels, the entire window area can become

a focal point of the room or act as a foil to a grouping of "hard" furnishings (such as a dining room table and chairs) or a masonry floor.

Shades

Fabric shades are another soft covering. They take up less space than most curtains and draperies and, because they require less fabric, can be more economical. Balloon, or Austrian, shades have a rather delicate, poufed appearance that fits a bedroom better than an office or a den; their gently curved folds are pleasing to the eye, but they are notorious dust catchers. Roman shades, on the other hand, have a more tailored look; when drawn, the fabric folds into soft horizontal pleats that are neat without looking pressed into place, and

they are easier to clean than Austrian shades.

There is also a variety of manufactured pleated fabric shades in different sizes and a wide selection of solid colors; the shades may be thin and translucent or backed with a material that insulates against heat and cold and resists damage from the sun.

Linings

To substantially extend the life of opaque fabric coverings, you can line them with a cotton backing; even in rooms that aren't subject to direct sunlight, the lining will help the material hang better and provide some insulation. Lining can help the appearance of windows from the outside, too; though your draperies or shades may vary in color and

pattern from room to room, the lining will give the appearance of uniformity and minimize unwanted contrast with the exterior of your home.

Other Ideas

With a little imagination, you can find creative alternatives to conventional drapery fabric. Sheets are one of the easiest materials to work with, and in a bedroom can be coordinated with bedding. An old lace tablecloth or a coverlet can lend a delicate, old-fashioned air to a room. If you come upon a remnant that's perfect for your decorating scheme but is too small for a full-sized window treatment, use it as a valance— alone or in combination with inexpensive ready-mades. If you do decide to purchase yardage for your coverings but

Without appearing too busy, neat, tailored Roman shades add softness and some pattern to this dining area.

you're not sure how the material will look, drape, or hang, buy a yard or two to experiment with. Whether or not you choose that particular fabric, you can always use it to cover toss pillows or a small tabletop.

Hardware

As you match your drapery plans to your budget, don't forget to allow for hardware, both decorative and functional. Some poles and rods are meant to be seen as well as to support your window dressings, and often carry decorative—and expensive—finials at each tip. If the pole or rod is to be hidden by fabric, you can buy an inexpensive one and create your own fancy effects by attaching finials available from hardware stores or home-improvement centers; if the pole is to show, you might consider covering its length with the same or a companion fabric for an eye-pleasing effect.

Nonfabric Shades, Blinds, and Shutters

Shades may be found in a number of materials other than fabric: natural-looking bamboo, trim matchsticks, crisp rice paper, airy woven grasses, and woven woods. They can be an excellent choice for windows that you want to blend into the background and for those that need minimal coverage. Shades take up little space, especially when they are set into the window frame, and almost seem to disappear when rolled up; they lend themselves to atypical windows, such as skylights and greenhouse panels. When used as the sole window covering, shades impart an understated, crisp look to a room, but they are easily paired with drapery treatments for a dressier mood.

What can be said of shades applies to blinds as well—both are versatile, low profile, and give a trim, crisp look. Horizontal blinds vary from narrow to wide slats, from ½-inch miniblinds to styles with louvers 2 inches wide or more. They may be painted, covered with fabric, or made of metal, wood, or vinyl. Vertical blinds, which open to the side much like draperies, offer nearly as many options in material and color as their horizontal counterparts, though they typically have wider louvers. Blinds offer one advantage over drapes or shades: The individual slats can be adjusted easily to regulate the amount of light entering a room.

Wood shutters lend a more solid architectural appearance to a window than most blinds; they, too, adjust easily to let in more or less light. Shutters can adopt an almost chameleon-like personality in a room. When they are painted or stained the same as the window frame, they appear to be an integral part of the window. When painted to match the surrounding walls as well, the shutters become part of the overall wall detailing; moreover, when their louvers are shut tight, the shutters seem to disappear into the background. Custom-cut shutters provide a close, neat fit and may be ordered with a finish to

Wood shutters suit almost any decor. They provide privacy yet allow in an adjustable amount of light.

complement the colors and style of your room. If your windows are of standard size, you may be able to purchase less expensive precut shutters to install and finish yourself.

Glass Doors

Finding a suitable window covering for glass doors presents some of the same challenges as dressing up windows. When a glass door lends drama or architectural impact to a space, it's preferable to leave it bare. When some covering is necessary, however, to provide privacy or control light, you can treat the door as a special-case window. French doors, like casement windows, respond best to individual matching treatments on each door. You can dress them in fabric coverings, such as shirred sheers stretched between rods secured at the top and bottom of the glass panes, or Roman shades, which, when pulled up, create a soft valance effect at the top of each door. Horizontal blinds and other types of shades are also appropriate for French doors.

Sliding glass doors offer different challenges. You can install floor-length draperies, curtains, or vertical blinds that draw out of the way in the same direction as the door slides. Alternatively, horizontal shades or blinds can be pulled up and concealed beneath a valance over the door. (A standard 6-foot slider will look fine with a single blind or shade; if the door is wider, or serves as part of a window wall, a set of two side-by-side blinds or shades may work better. A set also allows more flexible control of light and privacy.)

An Illustrated Glossary of Window Terms

Austrian shade This lightweight curtain fabric, when pulled up with a cord, gathers into soft scallops. Balloon shades are similar in design, but have a softer, more billowy appearance.

Finial Ornamental hardware used to decorate the ends of drapery or curtain rods or poles, finials may be simple brass spheres or wood tips or be custom-made to fit a particular window theme.

Jabot This vertical "tail," or fabric section, drapes down on either side of a swag or a valance.

Lambrequin A wooden frame built across the top of a window and down its sides to the floor, a lambrequin is typically covered with fabric, and intended to make the window appear larger or add architectural interest.

Roman shade Usually made from a medium-weight fabric, a Roman shade draws up into accordian-like horizontal pleats, resulting in a neat but not stiff folded covering.

Swag This graceful curve of fabric is shaped, looped, or simply draped across a window top. It may be folded to hide hardware or loosely draped to show off a decorative pole or curtains underneath.

Valance This horizontal treatment over the top of a window is used to conceal hardware or give a finished look to a window treatment. It may be of wood, fabric alone, or a fabric-covered board.

Finials

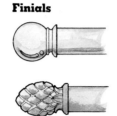
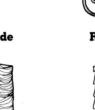

Austrian shade

Roman shade

Jabot

Swag

Lambrequin

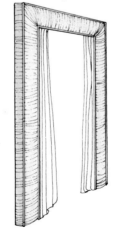

Valance

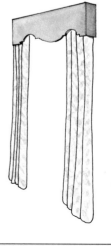

FURNISHINGS

This section presents ideas about reusing your present furnishings, offers guidelines for smart shopping for new pieces, discusses upholstery, and acquaints you with some of the furniture classics that have made an impact on interior decoration over the past 300 years.

What Do You Have?

In the chapter on "Planning Your Spaces," you worked on developing a furniture plan and room profile chart to assist in the all-important task of actually furnishing the spaces. Now is the perfect time to retrieve those plans (floor plan and elevations) and work sheets from your binder to review your intended furniture arrangements and notes. What did you plan to keep? Discard or move to another room? Have you changed your mind? Which pieces need to be refurbished in some way—repainted, recovered, refreshed with professional cleaning? What did you decide about the style and mood of the room? Does your choice still appeal to you? What are the essential furnishings you feel you need to purchase? Will you buy them new at a retail store, through a designer, or secondhand? What about the secondary items? Did you plan for any built-ins, or will your furnishings be mainly movable pieces?

Few homeowners can afford to fill a room with all-new furnishings—or want to, for that matter—so taking stock of what you have and showing it at its best is as important to the decorating process as incorporating something new. As you retrace your steps through the questions in the previous paragraph, consider each piece of furniture individually as well as within the room as a whole.

What Do You Need?

Deciding what type of furnishings will function best in any given situation is one dimension of planning for furniture needs. Another is figuring out how much seating and storage is needed, how many tables and work surfaces.

As you evaluate the types of furnishings you'll need for your room, think about function (or multifunction) first; next consider materials, maintenance, and comfort in light of your family living patterns; then consider aesthetics. As you window-shop for possible additions to your core of present furnishings, again think first about function, followed closely by quality—both in materials and construction. When you actually begin the furniture-selection process, assemble all of these criteria in a checklist to help you keep your priorities straight. After all, a sofa that draws your attention because the fabric is interesting and has the right colors for your scheme may not fill any of the other criteria. The sofa may be the wrong size for the space, uncomfortable, covered in a material that's hard to keep clean, and—beneath that pretty surface—poorly made.

Seating

Providing a variety of seating that can accommodate a number of users in a single room is probably the most workable approach to the perpetual problem of what's comfortable for one member of the family may not be comfortable for another. One alternative is to combine several types of seating to appease everyone: a standard-height sofa or love seat (14 to 18 inches), which will suit the average build, combined with a slightly lower and deeper armchair and ottoman and a couple of dining or side chairs with somewhat higher seats and straighter backs.

Modular seating, sometimes referred to as sectionals, offers flexibility in arranging and rearranging furnishings in a number of ways. Large modular groupings that have only two or three sections are less versatile than the smaller units, especially in rooms where supplementary furnishings also play a role, and large groupings typically look best in spacious settings. Matching armless chairs and ottomans can sometimes be arranged to resemble a modular unit—handy when you wish to create a temporary seating group for a particular function—and be moved back to their original places with a minimum of hassle.

Tables and Desks

Although tables and desks vary tremendously in appearance, size, shape, height, and material, they all serve one major function: They are the flat surfaces intended to put things down on, whether it's the breakfast dishes, a collection of mementos, lamps, books, a typewriter, or a tank of fish.

Most dining room and kitchen tables are 29 or 30 inches tall, but their shapes and dimensions vary with their designers. A few types of tables—game tables, conference-style tables, and folding card tables among them—are a little lower and can be a good choice for a family setting where old and young folk share activities at the same location. Being comfortable at a table often has as much to do with having enough elbow room as distance from the floor: 24 to 30 inches of edge space per person is recommended. If you plan to seat a maximum of four persons, for example, you can get away with a 36- to 42-inch-round table (30 to 42 inches if it's square); but if the group will number six, you'll need a 42- to 48-inch-round table (at least 40 by 48 inches if rectangular, preferably larger). Tables with extensions or leaves can give extra diners the elbow room they need.

Coffee tables are typically about 15 inches off the floor and seem to bridge the gap between a true table and a bench to prop your feet on while reading the evening newspaper. They're ideal for holding books, magazines, and coffee cups, and are most useful when they have a durable surface. A long coffee table in front of an equally long sofa can obstruct traffic, so you might consider substituting two smaller tables side by side.

The term *occasional table* usually refers to a table that stands next to or near a chair or the end of a sofa, or one that might rest against a wall. Like the occasional chair, it is not used on a regular basis but can be relied upon to fill an occasional need. If space is at a premium in your room, consider tables that stretch space visually, such as those made of glass or Plexiglas, or those that can be stacked in a nest or folded away.

Depending on the situation, a table may serve as a desk, and vice versa. Many of the requirements are similar. Since desks are intended primarily as table-like work surfaces, nearly all are manufactured at a standard height of 29 inches (sometimes 30 inches); computer or typewriter desks or tables are a few inches lower. If the height is uncomfortable for the user, the chair is adjusted with a mechanism that raises or lowers the seat. Many desks incorporate storage capabilities, a feature

that few tables offer, but, of course, a table can be converted into a desk with the addition of file cabinets or other storage systems underneath. Just remember to leave adequate leg room to move around comfortably.

Furniture for Storage

Most homes never seem to have enough closets or built-in cupboards or shelves, so storage space is often found in

Comfortable seating is an obvious priority in this charming living room.

Selecting Upholstered Furnishings

Some manufacturers supply furniture outlets with cutaway samples of the construction of upholstered pieces; others leave it up to the potential customer to figure out the inside story. The following guidelines will aid in your investigation as will the section on fabric selection (page 82).

Frame

The frame itself should be constructed from seasoned, kiln-dried hardwood; ash, birch, oak, hickory, poplar, and maple are often-used species. Joints must be sturdy and strong, preferably joined with double dowels or spiral-groove dowels that have been screwed and glued in place. Look for corners that have been reinforced with wood braces. Braces running front to back will add further strength. If the piece has been assembled so that none of these features is evident, ask to see the manufacturer's specifications and any other pertinent literature.

Legs

They should either be extensions of the frame itself or pieces of solid hardwood that have been joined securely with interlocking parts. Be wary of legs that have been screwed into the frame or attached with metal plates: They are typically weaker and often indicative of an inferior product.

Springs

Coil springs are the most familiar and durable spring and by far the best choice for seats. For quality, look for those that are hand-tied in an eight-way pattern (the tying runs from front to back, side to side, and diagonally—a method that provides good support and prevents sagging).

Sinuous, or S, springs, also made of wire, are less expensive to manufacture and install than coils. They are commonly used in the backs of upholstered furnishings, where not as much support is required.

The third spring system is a combination of S springs and heavy elastic bands that make up a strong, springy webbing. Used in European furnishings for some time, this webbing offers excellent support and is frequently found in imported pieces with a shallow seat.

Spring Cover

Better-quality pieces may have the springs sewn to a layer of burlap or canvas to help keep them in position. The fabric is fastened to the frame; typically another layer of canvas is stretched across the underside of the frame for a more finished appearance.

Padding

Foam rubber is most common, but padding can be of other materials as well—cotton batting, synthetics, or rubberized fibers. Has the padding been installed evenly and stitched or buttoned down so that it won't slip or lose shape with time and use? Check to see that padding covers not just the armrest but also the sides—an area where manufacturers sometimes skimp.

Cushions

Polyester fiberfill is the most widely used filling for back cushions. Other fillings include kapok, or a mixture of kapok and cotton; feathers or down, or a combination of the two; or a blend of cotton and hair (boar bristle is often used).

For seat cushions, one quality filling is a sandwichlike arrangement of heavy polyurethane foam wrapped with either polyester fiberfill or down.

Some manufacturers of quality furnishings, and many custom upholstery firms, offer a cushion that incorporates coil springs into its core: The springs are individually wrapped, tied together into a system, and then surrounded by a filling—polyurethane foam for a firm seat, down or feathers for a soft one.

---

dressers, chests, wardrobes, bookcases, and china cabinets. Like other furnishings, storage units must be assessed in terms of function, materials and construction, and cost. A durable painted chest or bureau, for example, will better suit a child's room than a fine hardwood chest of drawers. A metal or plywood cabinet might be a practical, inexpensive choice for the laundry, garage, or back hall, but something more aesthetically pleasing could house your fine china or dress up the front entry.

Storage systems offer a variety of components that fit together in any number of ways to solve storage needs. When placed against a wall, or used as partitions and dividers, storage components can take on the appearance of built-in furniture. Since new furnishings intended for storage are not inexpensive, take time and care in evaluating their workmanship and be certain that they truly meet your needs.

Shopping for Furnishings

The best way to get what you pay for is to become an informed and aggressive shopper. Once you have a fairly good idea of what you might buy, but before you make up your mind, visit a number of retail furniture outlets. The salespeople may think you're just browsing, but your goal is to put furnishings to the test. Sit, lean, bounce, shake, knock, push, pull (within reason, of course): New furniture should be up to the normal kind of wear and tear it will receive in your home.

Wherever feasible, turn the piece over to study its underside; closely examine such areas as joints and seams. Ask about construction, materials, warranties, fabrics, the manufacturer, and so forth, and don't be put off by a salesperson who hedges your questions or changes the subject. Find one who is knowledgeable—or go somewhere else. Although your budget

them revived from earlier periods, others innovative in design and application. Some are excessively ornate, others deceivingly plain in appearance.

Revival

The first style to be revived was the Gothic, originally conceived as an architectural application, and secondarily for furnishings. Victorian society often ignored the original intent and filled their homes with ordinary furnishings dressed up with pointed arches, tracery, and medieval carvings.

The most influential style of the mid-1800s, however, was the Rococo Revival, which literally took over Victorian parlors and sitting rooms with updated versions of Louis XV armchairs and elaborately carved marble-top tables. By the 1870s, the Renaissance Revival style emerged, often in the form of large cabinets and sideboards ornamented with carved and gilded surface decorations, and wood and mother-of-pearl inlay.

Metal, Wicker, Bentwood

Indoor and outdoor wrought-iron furniture, brass beds, and a variety of wicker pieces from this era are still functional and sought after in antique shops from coast to coast. As early as 1860 Americans were enjoying the fruits of a different sort of mass production in the classic bentwood chair, developed in Vienna by Michael Thonet and imported in tremendous quan-

tities. Thonet perfected a technique to bend solid wood with steam and created furnishings that were lightweight, strong, and inexpensive.

American Mission Style

Under the guidance of William Morris in England, and later Gustav Stickley in the United States, the Arts and Crafts Movement sought to counteract the Victorian tendency toward excess and the inferior workmanship of so many factory-produced items with an emphasis on quality and the return of the craftsman to the realm of furnishings. Fashioned primarily from oak, Mission-style furniture displays clean, rectangular lines and rather boxy proportions, and is well-suited to a variety of contemporary interiors.

Art Nouveau

The first Art Nouveau designs of the 1890s were designed in reaction to the prevailing Victorian decoration. Art Nouveau as applied to furnishings usually refers to the French form, characterized by flowing lines, rhythmic asymmetric patterns, and stylized naturalistic motifs somewhat Japanese in their references. By abandoning historical references, this "new art" was a genuinely modern style.

Twentieth Century

The growth of industrialism and technology in the twentieth century introduced materials

beyond traditionally used woods, and architects and designers were among the first to fashion these machine-made materials into furniture. Their goals were to create furnishings that were simple, functional, free from tradition, and easy to mass-produce commercially.

Early Modern

Marcel Breuer made history in 1928 with a cantilevered chair that seemed to float freely above the floor: Its bent tubular steel frame supported a lightweight cane seat and back without the help of conventional legs. A year later, Mies van der Rohe introduced his Barcelona chair, a comfortable leather-cushioned design with a graceful X-shaped frame modeled on seats common in ancient Greece and Rome. In the early 1930s, Finnish designer Alvar Aalto created another sensation with a sculptural wood armchair, its flowing seat and back constructed from a single sheet of molded and laminated birch plywood, its arms from ribbonlike plywood loops.

Art Deco

The 1920s and 1930s were also marked by a different kind of modern movement in furniture design, Art Deco, which sought to integrate the spareness and purity of industrial design with cultural motifs, and express them in both traditional and new materials. Designed with an eye to function, Art Deco furnishings were often squat in shape but sleek of line, with

plain lacquered or veneered surfaces. Many pieces featured bold simplified geometric patterns, sometimes achieved through contrasting woods or by alternating the direction of the grain of veneers.

Recent Modern

The innovative functional furnishings of Marcel Breuer and his contemporaries influenced later designers. In the 1950s Charles Eames became admired for his lounge chair and ottoman and his deceivingly simple desk and side chair, both made from molded plywood. Eero Saarinen was recognized for his molded plastic pedestal chair. More recently, a number of lesser-known designers have created comfortable, functional, aesthetically pleasing furnishings that suit a variety of decorating styles.

Today

The close of the twentieth century is seeing a renaissance of sorts in American furniture-making, a melding of technology and tradition. Just as eighteenth-century cabinet-makers revised English patterns to fit their materials and needs, a large segment of today's furniture makers are reinterpreting traditional styles in their own designs. In time, their pieces will likely find a place in history and homes as everyday classics.

FABRICS FOR FURNISHINGS

Fabrics play a major role in the home—on windows; sometimes on walls, ceilings, and floors; and on many furnishings. Versatile, economical, functional, and available in a tremendous range of colors, patterns, and textures, fabric can't be beat as a decorative tool and a protective covering.

Fabric Basics

In past centuries, especially in grand houses filled with architectural embellishments, fabrics were placed on walls and floors to muffle sound and insulate against the cold but less frequently on furnishings themselves. Fabrics were seldom regarded for their decorative potential. But today's interiors have inherited little architectural splendor, and fabric can go a long way to lift a room from ordinary to unique.

Actually, the word *fabric* is an encompassing term, referring to basically anything manufactured by hand or machine that is somewhat pliable or supple: cloths, rugs, carpet, cane, rush—even paper and wire fencing. Textiles are fabrics that have been woven by hand or machine, although some people use the term loosely to mean any fabric made from natural or synthetic fibers. Fibers are strong, flexible, threadlike filaments twisted into strands of yarn of varying lengths, and then typically woven or knitted into fabric. (Sometimes, fibers are processed into films or sheets rather than into yarns.)

Natural fibers, which are derived from plant and animal substances, must be cleaned, spun, and stretched out before being made into yarn; man-made fibers emerge from the machine as clean, continuous filaments ready to go. Traditionally, natural fibers, such as cotton, silk, and wool, have been favored as fabrics for the home, but a whole generation of synthetics—and especially blends of natural and man-made fibers—are now providing materials that rate high in performance, looks, and economy.

Selecting Fabric

As you know from visiting furniture showrooms, the first things to notice about any fabric are its color and pattern, then its apparent and actual texture. Of course, selecting an upholstery fabric involves much more than first impressions. Is it a practical material for the type of furnishing in question and for the room the piece will occupy? What fiber is it made from, and how is it constructed? What sort of finish does the fabric have— soil resistant, moth repellent, flame-retardant? Will the fiber, weave, and finish all hold up under heavy use? How about cost and maintenance? Choosing the right fabric will not only extend the life of your furniture, it will also make your own life easier.

Texture, Pattern, Color

Nearly everything that goes into the makeup of fabric influences its texture—the way the yarn is spun, the natural characteristics of the fiber, the weaving techniques, the density. Think about the feel and appearance of cotton: sheers at the window, chintz on the

Fabrics provide the drama in this sophisticated family room. The strong flame pattern on the chair and pillow is matched visually by the rich forest green used to cover the sofa and windows.

pillows, corduroy on the family-room sofa, canvas on the patio chairs. Fabrics can be transparent or opaque or somewhere in between; they can feel smooth, rough, slick, ridged, or fuzzy. Some can feel uncomfortably prickly, itchy, slippery, or sticky (as with some vinyls); others can feel plush, satiny, or soft.

Pattern, like texture, enlivens the look and feel of fabric, but the sensation is a visual one. If your room will have few furnishings, you can play up the fabric pattern on upholstered pieces; if a number of objects will be showcased, you can combine subtle prints with a few stronger ones, tying them together with color or a theme. Striped patterns, for instance, can be used almost anywhere (as can plaids and checks, which are really variations on the stripe) and act as effective transitions between plain fabrics and bolder ones. Some patterns are printed directly on the fabric surface, as is true of many cottons and linens; others are woven into the material itself and may appear on both sides of the fabric, making it reversible; still other patterns are intricately woven to produce a raised relief that creates actual as well as visual texture.

Color is as important a characteristic as pattern and texture. Dyeing is the primary means of bringing color to fabric. The textile may be dyed after weaving, a process which usually results in a solid-color fabric. When the yarns are dyed first, and then woven together, many variations in color and pattern are possible. Dyed fabrics, however, are fairly susceptible to fading in the sun and to losing some of their color during washing or dry cleaning.

Colors may also be printed on fabric in a variety of ways. One of the most common methods used today is screen printing—a process used in coloring wallpaper as well. A screen of finely woven fabric is employed for each color to be applied; each screen is designed to block out any areas where the color is not to appear, so that when the pigment or dye is forced through the screen onto the fabric, it colors only the intended area. Hand-screening is labor intensive, so that fabrics printed this way are expensive. Most fabric manufacturers use a faster, more economical mechanical rotary process to do screen printing.

Natural Fibers

As already noted, the fibers that are fashioned into yarn may be natural or man-made. Natural fibers are derived from both plant and animal substances and are noted for their strength. In the plant category, cotton, linen, and burlap are the best known.

Cotton, in particular, is extremely versatile, and the most commonly used fiber in a large number of fabrics—by itself or in combination with other fibers. It resists abrasion, cleans easily, takes color and finishes well, and is relatively inexpensive. Heavyweight cotton makes an excellent upholstery material. On the other hand, cotton wrinkles, burns easily, and fades in the sun.

Linen, a more costly fiber, holds its shape well and holds up better in the sun (although it also burns and wrinkles very easily), but because it lacks resiliency and needs special care to keep it looking fresh and at its best, linen is not the best choice for upholstery.

Animal Fibers

Wool is the most highly regarded animal fiber. It can be described in mostly positive terms: elastic, resilient, and strong; resistant to soils and stains and easy to clean (with proper attention); and insulating against heat and cold (the springy coil of the sheep's hair, from which wool comes, traps air and acts as a natural insulator). Furthermore, wool doesn't burn readily. Its major drawback is expense, and the fact that moths love the fabric as much as (or even more than) people. Fortunately, special treatments and the availability of wool-synthetic blends have reduced both the price and potential moth damage.

Mohair, a type of wool derived from the hair of the angora goat, shares many of the same qualities as sheep wool and in its heavier forms has become increasingly popular as an upholstery fabric; it is more expensive than most sheep wool, but less than many silks.

Silk, unraveled from the cocoon of the silkworm, remains the most luxurious of fabrics, at once lustrous and elastic, resistant to soiling and burns but fragile in the presence of sunlight—and very costly. Silk is used in heavy upholstery fabrics, such as damask and brocade. (You can read more about cloths made from these fibers in the chart on page 82.)

Synthetics

Some synthetics are better than others as upholstery fabrics. Selecting a blend of synthetic and natural fibers can provide the best of both worlds—and many manufacturers have met that demand. Here is a comparison of the more common synthetics used in home furnishings.

Rayon and acetate are both derived from wood pulp, which is then chemically processed into a synthetic material. Both fibers are sometimes used as an economical substitute for silk because they drape well and can have a silky appearance (rayon can be made to resemble a number of fibers, including linen); but neither is as strong as its natural counterpart and weakens further in sunlight. Acetate in particular burns readily and will melt. Rayon-wool blends are often used for upholstery fabrics.

Acrylics offer wool-like qualities and textures without the cost (or the moths). Not as strong as wool, with a tendency to pill and to stretch with time, acrylics nonetheless have many attributes: elasticity, resiliency, low burn rate, color retention (even in sunlight), and relatively easy maintenance.

Polyester, too, can be silk- or wool-like. Although strong, elastic, and largely wrinkle free, polyester fibers have a slithery texture and don't take dye easily. Generally too light a fiber for upholstery needs, polyester-cotton blends are commonly used as window dressings.

Nylon has been around for some time and is often blended with other fibers for home use. Nylon is very strong and resilient, resists abrasion well, and can even be sponge-cleaned. Because the fiber has a glassy appearance that doesn't show furnishings at their best, however, nylon is usually blended with wool in upholstery fabrics.

Although many fabrics are constructed from other man-made fibers, and some from metal and glass fibers as well, they are typically too light, too fragile, or simply inappropriate for upholstery use, and will not be covered here.

Types of Weaves

Most fabrics use yarn as their basic element and are con-structed through some type of weaving process. The most common construction is a two-element weave, and among these, the plain weave is the most familiar. Evident in fabrics from cheesecloth to taffeta, it utilizes the technique of over-and-under interlacing of length-wise yarns (the warp) and horizontal yarns (the weft, or filling)—the same weave your children used on those cherished potholders hanging on the kitchen wall. By varying the tex-tures and colors of the arrange-ment of over-and-under yarns, a number of different patterns can be created. A variation on the plain weave is the basket weave, which also uses two elements but varies the interlacing tech-nique: canvas, duck, and sail-cloth are examples.

The plain weave can be-come less plain with the addi-tion of a third element, which adds some relief to the fabric surface, as in a brocade. When the third element projects above the surface in loops, the result is a pile weave, which may be cut (velour and velvet), uncut (terrycloth), or a com-bination of both (corduroy). Adding elements can create double cloths, which often show different colors and pat-terns on each side, or face, and fabrics with quilted effects.

Twill weaves carry the hori-zontal weft strands over one or more and under two or more warp yarns in a progressive but shifting sequence that creates a diagonal effect. Two-element twill weaves include herring-bone and denim; three- or four-element twills can be made into heavy brocades and tweeds.

Another basic weaving tech-nique is the satin weave, in which the warp floats over four or more weft strands and under one at regular or staggered in-tervals to create a compact, un-broken surface. Since the yarns are packed more closely than in many other weaves, the fabric has a smooth, often lustrous, surface. Satin and damask are woven in this way.

The terms *Jacquard weave* and *Jacquard fabric* are fre-quently used among fabric manufacturers to indicate a style of weave that's intricate in design and three-dimensional in texture, but the word *Jac-quard* actually refers to the loom used to produce the fabric rather than to the weave or the cloth itself. A number of heavy-weight upholstery fab-rics, such as tapestries, bro-cades, damasks, and some velvets, are woven on a Jac-quard loom.

Shopping for Fabrics

Think of fabric as a six-way material: front, back, and four directions to the face (up, down, and side to side). Exam-ine each dimension closely for flaws in fiber, weave, backing, and quality of selvage (the side

A little bit of fabric can add a lot of decorating impact if used in the right places.

A Word About Finishes

Before fabrics leave the mill, they sometimes undergo one or more processes, or finishes, to make them more resistant to the various hazards they might encounter in the typical home. Though largely chemical in nature, these finishes seldom weaken, stiffen, or change the color and appearance of the fabric itself. In addition to finishes that protect against fire, stains, and soil, finishes have also been developed to combat insects, mildew, molds, and fungus. Wool and wool blends have benefited from treatments to discourage moths; cotton and linen, from treatments to shed wrinkles; and cotton and rayon, finishes to repel water.

Fire Retardants

Fabrics constructed from animal fibers—wool, silk, and mohair (and leather and suede, which are fabrics derived from animal hide)—are difficult to ignite, and burn slowly. They are considered naturally flame resistant. Glass and metal fibers are actually fireproof, or nonflammable. The dangers occur with the plant-based fibers, which are flammable, and most of the synthetic fibers, which not only burn but often melt.

Although you may come upon some fabrics that have been chemically fireproofed, it's more likely you'll encounter finishes that are fire retardant (treated chemically to resist ignition and retard flame spread) or flame resistant (chemically treated to resist just ignition). Check the label or the manufacturer's specifications to find out whether the finish is rated fire retardant, whether it is durable (guaranteed to last through so many washings and dry cleanings), and whether it is built into the fabric or applied topically.

Soil and Stain Resistants

A growing number of upholstery fabrics now receive a soil- and stain-resistant finish at the factory rather than as a topical application to the completed furniture. Applied sooner or later, however, these finishes certainly do help, slowing down the absorption rates of liquids, for instance, and making it harder for dirt and dust to permeate the fabric surface. But they only protect—not prevent—and regular vacuuming and prompt removal of spills will lengthen the life of both fabric and finish.

After you identify the brand name of the particular finish, find out the chemical company's recommendations for cleaning and care. Some repellents may react with certain cleaning fluids, for instance, releasing dye or making the stain more noticeable, or they may develop fine cracks that allow the soil to penetrate the finish. Some finishes will repel only water-borne stains; others resist both water- and oil-based stains. If you are ordering upholstered furnishings, be sure that the furniture manufacturer or upholsterer provides all the necessary information on the fabric, whether it's included on the label or in a separate spot- and stain-removal guide.

---

edges that are meant to keep the fabric from unraveling). Handle the fabric; put it to the test to check pliability, draping quality, strength, tendency to wrinkle, shape retention, and potential for snagging, fuzzing, and pilling. Note how the fabric feels. Is it comfortable against the skin? Does it prickle or itch when you rub it? Does it feel wet or cold?

Look closely at the fibers and their construction. Determine from the label on a sample or on the bolt the fiber content, type of weave, resistance to abrasion (many fabrics undergo an abrasion test administered at the mill), special finishes, recommended maintenance, and color retention.

What about the pattern? Is it printed on the surface or is it an integral part of the weaving process? If the fabric has a repeating pattern, or a design that must be matched, be aware that you'll need to buy additional yardage. Study the pattern and weave to see if you can "railroad" the fabric—that is, turn it on its side—in order to run vertical stripes in a horizontal direction, for instance.

Once you're satisfied that the fabric meets all your needs, take a large sample home to view it in the surroundings where it will be used. Keep it for a few days to be certain it's really what you want. Remember, no matter how much you like the color and appearance, don't lose sight of how and where it will be used. Remember, too, that no fabric does it all: Some will wear for years but feel uncomfortable against the skin, or lack aesthetic appeal; few resist fading in the sun; and virtually none can resist the ravages of soil.

When you're ready to order the fabric, bring the *exact* dimensions of the object to be covered (and a snapshot, if possible) to the fabric store. Since fabrics come in a variety of widths, from 36 inches to 60 inches—and patterns can repeat as much as every 18 inches or more—you'll need to get an accurate figure to purchase the right quantity. Don't forget to allow for skirts, pleats, welts, pillows, arm covers, and so on. If you'll be bringing the material to your own upholsterer, this person can calculate for you exactly how much to buy.

Purchase all the fabric at one time to guarantee that it comes from the same dye lot, and buy a little extra as a safety measure.

Finally, if the fabric doesn't carry a stain- and soil-resistant finish, seriously consider having one applied to the completed piece at the factory or upholstery house. Investing a few extra dollars in a special finish can extend the life of the piece.

A Sampler of Upholstery Fabrics

As you shop for fabrics, you'll find that they are often organized and displayed by category. The following fabrics, illustrated in the photograph on the opposite page, are the most common types.

Brocade A rich, rather ornate cloth with a raised pattern, brocade is usually woven on a Jacquard loom; it is traditionally made of silk but also silk-synthetic blends.

Canvas A heavy, sturdy, plain-weave cotton, canvas is suitable for outdoor furnishings; it is sometimes made of linen for indoor use. Duck and sailcloth are similar in weave and fiber but lighter in weight.

Chenille A tufted, cut-pile fabric of cotton or synthetics, chenille is constructed from a yarn of the same name. It is soft and slightly fuzzy to the touch, medium weight, and reversible; it is recommended for slipcovers, but not for households with cats, since the clipped pile snags readily.

Chintz A glazed-cotton fabric, usually with a glossy finish, chintz is typically patterned (floral prints are common); its light weight makes it a borderline choice for furnishings that will be subjected to heavy wear.

Corduroy A heavy-duty, durable cotton or cotton-synthetic blend, corduroy is distinguished by a pile cut that results in a ribbed or ridged texture.

Cretonne A plain- or twill-woven printed cotton fabric, cretonne is similar to chintz in appearance but heavier in weight and unglazed; it is a good substitute for chintz where prints are desirable.

Damask A delicately patterned cotton or silk fabric, damask resembles brocade but without a raised surface; its flat, Jacquard-style pattern results from combining two weaves. It is fully reversible, and available in a range of medium to heavy weights.

Denim A sturdy and serviceable twill-woven cotton cloth, denim has a tight twill weave with a diagonal pattern that gives the fabric a ridged appearance; drill is similar to denim but heavier and is typically gray in color.

Flannel A soft, medium-weight cloth with a slight nap to its surface, flannel is traditionally made from wool but is available in cotton and blends; it gets its raised texture from a bristled roller used during fabrication.

Gingham A lightweight but sturdy pure cotton (or cotton-synthetic blend), gingham is woven from dyed yarns into a series of simple patterns, such as stripes, plaids, and checks; it is often used for slipcovers.

Hopsacking A coarse, heavy, open-weave cloth of cotton or cotton blends, hopsacking is extremely durable; it is used almost exclusively for upholstery.

Matelassé A Jacquard-woven heavy cotton double cloth, matelassé is made with a pattern that resembles a quilted or puckered surface.

Mohair A sturdy and durable medium-weight fabric, mohair is made from the hair of the angora goat (usually mixed with cotton or wool); depending on the mixture of yarns and the weaving process, it may have a pattern woven into the fabric.

Needlepoint A heavy fabric, needlepoint is usually made from wool; when hand-embroidered, the wool is embroidered over a canvas or a net backing; the Jacquard loom can construct fabrics that simulate needlepoint.

Ottoman A heavy, densely woven fabric, ottoman has a distinctive horizontal pattern of wide, flat ribs; it is constructed from warp yarns of silk, acetate, or rayon and weft yarns of cotton or wool. Ottoman is extremely durable and well-suited for furnishings that receive heavy use.

Plastic sheeting or film A vinyl or polyvinyl chloride (PVC) nonwoven fabric used to simulate leather, plastic sheeting often has a cloth backing.

Plush A woven, heavy-pile cloth, plush is typically made from wool or mohair, or from synthetics, with a higher but less dense pile than velvet.

Rep A plain-woven, horizontally ribbed fabric, rep is very similar to ottoman but with its ribs rounded and more closely spaced.

Satin A smooth, glossy, lightweight, and luxurious-looking fabric, satin is usually woven from silk fibers but sometimes from synthetics; although it may be used for draperies, satin is not a good choice for most upholstery. Sateen, similar in appearance, is woven from cotton and is a much sturdier substitute.

Tapestry A heavy, hand-woven, or Jacquard-woven fabric made from wool, cotton, or linen, tapestry is nearly always strongly patterned and multicolored; the traditional flame stitch is found in tapestries, as are pictorial scenes.

Ticking A medium-weight cotton or linen cloth, ticking is widely used as a mattress and pillow covering and is characterized by a blue stripe against a white or cream background. The sturdiness of ticking has made it popular for upholstery and slipcovers, and it is now available with stripes of different colors.

Tweed A heavy, rough-textured fabric, tweed is made from wool or wool blends and typically twill woven: its characteristic mixed colors come from the yarn itself; the striped, checked, and herringbone patterns come from the twill weave.

Velour A heavy, durable fabric, velour has a short-pile or napped surface that resembles velvet; it is constructed from a variety of fibers, notably cotton.

Velvet A rich, luxurious-looking and -feeling fabric, velvet has a short, soft, dense cut or uncut loop pile, often of silk; its surface shows wear readily. Velveteen, made from cotton or synthetics, is similar in appearance but less luxurious and far more durable.

LIGHTING SYSTEMS

Everyone needs natural light to remain psychologically and physically healthy. And though we could all probably survive without the benefits of artificial lighting, the enjoyment of our homes and the vitality of its spaces would be greatly diminished.

What is Possible?

Making changes to an existing lighting system presents something of a dilemma to the homeowner. On the one hand, artificial lighting is an important design element: It can be used to emphasize some objects and de-emphasize others; enhance patterns, forms, and textures; enlarge spaces visually with brighter, more even illumination. Like natural light, artificial lighting can affect the appearance of colors and influence moods, making a room seem an efficient workplace or a cozy retreat, feel warm or cool, understated or dramatic.

At the same time, lighting systems are not as easily altered or put into place as a new coat of paint. Typically, redoing the lighting plan involves some structural changes—opening up the ceiling (and perhaps the walls) to rewire and replace fixtures—and incurring the costs that go with a remodeling project. And though a new lighting system may be worth the expense in the long term because it improves the aesthetics and the value of your home, decoratively speaking it may not have the instant impact, or satisfaction, of a change in color scheme or new carpet.

As you consider your decorating options, you might decide to explore the pros and cons of a new lighting system. You might choose to upgrade a home office with recessed ceiling fixtures, for instance, but simply add a floor lamp or two to the living room to improve its overall illumination and create a different mood. The key to better lighting is variety—a balance of general illumination, localized lighting for reading or tasks, and accent lighting—and an understanding of the ways in which lamps and fixtures can be arranged and sized for a particular space.

Lighting plays a critical role in this contemporary living room and is as important to the success of the room design as any of the furnishings.

Basic Types of Home Lighting

Comfortable, practical, and pleasing lighting derives from a combination of three basic types of illumination: general, task, and accent. How much of each to use varies with the room and its functions. A laundry/sewing room, for example, probably won't require decorative or accent lighting, whereas a dining room may depend on it to set a special mood.

General

Also known as background, or ambient, lighting, general lighting provides a low-to-moderate level of illumination for a particular area or room, bright enough to see people and objects clearly, but not uncomfortably bright. Ambient lighting typically works best when a number of light sources are used together: ceiling and wall fixtures; floor and table lamps; uplights and down-lights, which shine light upward or down. The overall effect can become monotonous or flat, however, if all of the fixtures give off the same amount of light, so varying the intensities around the room is recommended. General illumination may be direct, as when the source of light is visible; or indirect, as when the fixture is concealed behind some sort of baffle that deflects the light in a particular direction.

Task

By contrast, task, or localized, lighting provides adequate and suitable light to carry out specific activities, such as reading the newspaper, assembling a model airplane, applying makeup, or paring vegetables. Whether the fixture is hanging, setting on a table or shelf, or directed downward from the ceiling, it is intended to illuminate the work surface or the task at hand.

Accent

This type of lighting, also called decorative lighting, draws the eye to objects or areas of the room that merit special attention—a display on the mantel, a painting, an exotic plant. Sometimes, accent lighting is used to make an impact, or set up a contrast, and its drawing power may come from strong, focused light directed on a specific item or place. Sometimes, the accent is on aesthetics, on creating a mood, or attracting the eye to a display of accessories, such as a collection of old family photographs or a dramatic plant.

Light and Mood

You can change the entire mood of a room by replacing standard light bulbs with colored ones, or by tucking a piece of theatrical gel (the colored filters used on stage lights) between bulb and shade. You can dramatize a shelf wall with a series of lights installed in creative ways—possibly strings of mini lights hidden under the shelves or a miniature-track system mounted on the ceiling.

Varying the color of light is another way to create interest and alter the mood of a space. There are several things you can do besides changing the bulb to one of a different color. You can begin with altering the wattage: A conventional 60-watt light bulb, for instance, gives off a medium-yellow glow; when it's dimmed moderately, it takes on a golden cast that becomes progressively more amber the dimmer it gets. (A 25-watt bulb also has an amber glow.) Quartz-halogen lamps, on the other hand, give off a bright white light; fluorescents can range from pinkish to greenish blue.

If you do wish to change the color of the bulb, though, well-stocked lighting stores offer several choices. Whether you alter the colors just a bit, or make a bolder statement, try to include three different tones. These variations in pattern, level of illumination, and color give a rhythm to the lighting plan that's pleasing to the eye and unifying to the overall room design.

A Personal Lighting Plan

If improving your present lighting system is on the agenda, it will pay in more ways than one to know exactly what you have in mind before you shop. Fixtures are expensive items; and though you might be able to return a floor lamp that doesn't fit your needs, any fixture you install will likely be yours for keeps. Assessing exactly what you want the lighting to accomplish, why you need it and where, and how much you can spend are the first concerns. Review the functions of the room yet again as well.

Chart it Out

Once you've thought over the ways your room will benefit from a change in lighting, it's time once again to peruse your final floor plan and elevations. If you don't have spare photocopies, make more.

Beginning with general lighting, sketch in the areas where you'd like to see the light pool, or flow across the walls, or fill a corner. Think about how you'd get the light to those areas and indicate it on your plans. You might feel that the best way to illuminate the primary seating area is from a track system on the ceiling that has two or three of its fixtures directed on that particular spot, and that the ideal way to brighten the corner is from a torchère-style floor lamp that casts light onto nearby walls.

As a next step, find all the areas on the plan where task lighting will be required and sketch in the fixtures you have in mind for the job, including any existing lamps you intend to reuse that are not already on the furniture plan. Finally, indicate any accent lighting you hope to incorporate. As you go through the steps, try to determine where you'd like the light source in plain view and where you'd prefer to have it hidden. (It might be helpful to use a different-color pencil for each type of lighting to see more clearly the pattern each takes and the areas where they overlap.)

Get Information

Gather your sketches together (and any pictures you've collected of lamps and fixtures that appeal to you) and visit a few lighting specialty stores. You might also take along some unmarked copies of your furniture plans. Many lighting centers have a consultant on staff who can answer specific questions and help map out a system for your room. If the lighting arrangement you've planned on paper will be too costly to implement, the consultant may be able to suggest alternatives.

It's also a good idea to visit a lighting laboratory in your area. Lighting labs provide an opportunity to compare different types of bulbs and see their range of color, dispersal of light, relative sizes, and so forth. These labs also display various setups for track, recessed, and fluorescent systems, and frequently show a number of solutions for combining the various types of lighting in specific areas of the home. (Some commercial and residential lighting dealers have a lighting lab within their facility but separate from the showroom. Check the Yellow Pages.)

Be Flexible

When the time comes to select the actual lighting for your design, you may have to make some compromises. If your budget doesn't allow the purchase of a track system and new table and floor lamps, for instance, it may be wiser to invest in track lighting and use other sources for finding the lamps—secondhand shops, rummage and estate sales, or inexpensive import shops. You can always replace the interim lamps when the occasion arises—at a closeout sale or with discontinued models—or when you can afford what you really desire.

Evaluating Light Fixtures

Light fixtures come in all shapes and sizes; many are flexibly designed to work in any given situation to solve a variety of problems. A hanging lamp over a dining room table can provide the necessary illumination in addition to providing ambient light and contributing to the decorative mood of the room; a well-positioned uplight can assist in general illumination by bouncing light off the ceiling or walls while accenting a sculptural plant. But function is only one of the factors in choosing the fixture that's best for the situation; the decision also depends on initial cost, appearance, ease of installation and maintenance, energy efficiency, and operating expenses.

For practical purposes, fixtures may be thought of as architectural (fixed in place or built into the structure itself);

or portable (movable devices that can be positioned and repositioned as furniture arrangements and redecorating instincts dictate). Recessed lighting is clearly architectural—and permanent; table lamps are definitely portable. A number of fixtures fall into either category. Track lighting and wall sconces, for instance, are installed directly against the ceiling or wall but are semipermanent because they can be removed relatively easily, even though the surface will have to be patched and repainted.

Ceiling and Wall Fixtures

Although hanging lamps and chandeliers will always have a place illuminating the dining room and breakfast areas of homes, hanging lamps in particular lend themselves to a variety of other situations. They are especially useful wherever downlighting is desirable for tasks; a reflector lining in the shade concentrates the beam even more and can be used to accent. Sometimes called pendant lamps, these fixtures range from the simple cord-hung metal shade to hi-tech chrome and glass versions, from Art Deco styles to Tiffany reproductions. The key to their placement is that the light from the bottom of the bulb (or bulbs) not create glare, or shine directly in the eye. Traditional chandeliers, too, need proper positioning to avoid creating unflattering shadows.

Track lighting is one of the most versatile of systems and

can be indispensable when decorating or redecorating. It can be mounted on almost any ceiling or wall, regardless of the material, and arranged in almost any configuration. The individual fixtures come in a number of sizes and finishes and can often accept a variety of bulbs. A track system may be employed to solve all the lighting needs of a room: Some fixtures work together to flood walls with even light for general illumination, others can be positioned to assist tasks, and still others to pinpoint the accents. Finally, if you wish, the system can be dismantled if you move and configured in a new space.

Wall fixtures range from practical cylinders that shine light up or down or in both directions, to decorative sconces that are usually designed to provide general indirect lighting rather than a focused beam. Wall sconces are available in a number of shapes, styles, and price ranges; some models are finely crafted and meant to enhance a wall like a work of art—and carry the price tag to prove it.

Table and Floor Lamps

These portable light fixtures serve an important role in a room: They bring comfort as well as convenience to the space, and they are at once functional and decorative.

Your selection process can go smoothly if you keep a few things in mind. Whether the lamp stands on the floor or sits on a table, its base and shade form a visual unit and should relate to each other in pleasing

Floor Plan With Furniture and Lights

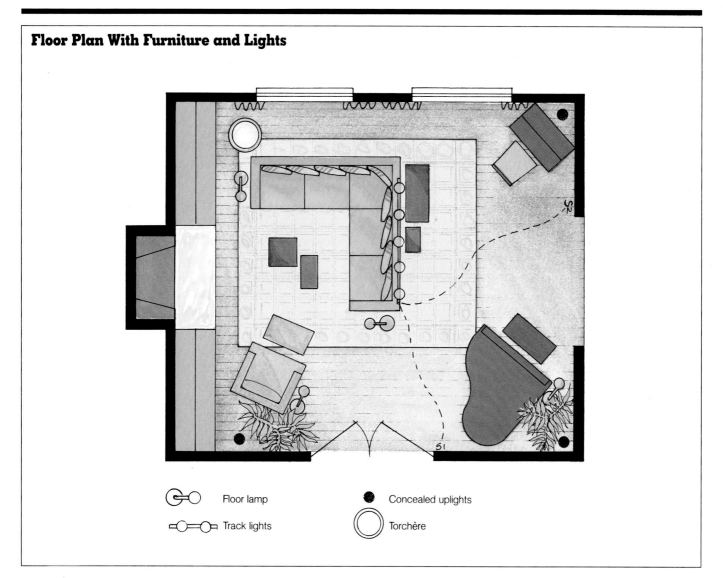

Floor lamp		Concealed uplights	
Track lights		Torchère	

ways. If the shade is proportionately too large for the base, the lamp will look top-heavy; if too small and high, the shade will appear to perch on the base, and the bulb may be exposed. In addition, the lamp as a whole should relate to nearby furnishings—neither seem too bulky for the table it sets on, nor dwarfed by the armchair it stands beside—and fit into the context of the room as a whole.

Once you've narrowed the field of lamps to a few final candidates, examine each closely for workmanship and materials. Quality lamps should have nonvisible joints and be constructed of heavy-gauge metals. Glass, ceramic, or wood bases should be heavy, stable, and well made. Check both electric cord and plug: Are they securely and safely fastened in place? Does the switch turn easily and feel sturdy? Does the fixture have a dimmer or three-way switch for energy savings? Does the light shine

up or down or in both directions? Will the lamp contribute to the general lighting of the room or function simply for task work?

Think about the lamp from a decorative standpoint, too. In a room setting, the base will probably be the first part of the fixture noticed because that's where most of the light falls. Is the color, texture, shape, and height to your liking and compatible with the room's design? The eye will move to the shade

next. Is it of the proper shape and scale for the base? What about the material? Fine pleats are delicate and traditional in style, but they are hard to keep clean. Translucent shades let a measure of light pass through, but their color will vary with the material and the intensity of the bulb; opaque shades, on the other hand, will seem darker when the light is on.

In the end, of course, no matter how much the lamp appeals to you aesthetically, it has to fulfill your lighting needs and fit into your budget.

FINISHING TOUCHES

However well planned and attractively decorated, no room feels complete without accessories, for it is these touches that underscore the personality of the space and reflect the taste of the family who uses it. Artwork as an accessory deserves special mention; a discussion of how to display your favorite pieces is covered in depth in this section.

Part of the Plan

Although accessories are usually introduced after the furniture has been placed, they shouldn't be regarded as afterthoughts. They have an important role as supplemental furnishings that round out the room and enrich the other objects in the space.

As such, they can be thought about and planned for in the same way you looked into other aspects of your decorating project. Large plants, a focal-point painting, sizable sculpture, or a grouping of photographs are all best considered as you develop your room design and draw up your floor and furniture plans.

Choosing the finishing touches that mean the most to you and your family is very personal. It may center around displaying artwork, artifacts, or antique candle holders. It may focus on creating tabletop arrangements of family photographs, lining shelves with mementos from travels abroad, or filling a glass-front cabinet with grandmother's irreplaceable china. Your room may be sparked by fresh flowers that change with the seasons, or from delicate dried arrangements that have timeless appeal. Its personality may come from quilts or fabrics that hang on the wall, from stained glass windows, or from sculpture.

Accessories can be anything you want them to be. They are the details that can pull together the many elements that make up the decor of your home.

Accessories can be decorative or practical, or both. Most serve in a decorative capacity, whether they supplement the major furnishings of the room, relate to the colors and textures of the space, or express the individuality of the owner: toss pillows on the sofa, a plant on a bookshelf, a display of personal treasures on a side table. Though the room might seem less complete without them, they are not necessary to the function of the space. Some accessories, however, have a practical role, and without them the enjoyment and use of the room would be hindered. Lamps fall into this category, as do tableware, bath towels, and bedding. Naturally, these accessories are most versatile when they are visually attractive as well as functional.

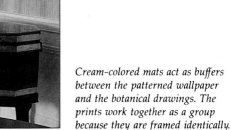

Cream-colored mats act as buffers between the patterned wallpaper and the botanical drawings. The prints work together as a group because they are framed identically.

As you approach the final stages of planning and developing your room design, keep your eyes open for a wide variety of items to accessorize and enrich your home. Look for personal belongings that you tucked away and forgot about; gather together all the photos lying loose in desk drawers; think about displaying your collection of antique bottles, shells and rocks, or African violets. If you wish to incorporate new purchases, attend craft fairs, visit galleries, and explore specialty boutiques, second-hand bookstores, and antique shops. Keep in mind that accessories, whether existing or new, will be more meaningful if they have a personal connection as well as a place in your decorating scheme.

Art and Photographs

As discussed in this book, *artwork* is a broad term that encompasses original paintings, fine-art prints, folk art, posters, and photographs. (It could be expanded to include other items as well.) Accessorizing with artwork can be either costly or economical: A one-of-a-kind original oil painting is usually an expensive investment and probably deserves a place of honor in your home; limited-edition prints that have been signed by the artist are less costly to purchase but can make just as valuable a statement on your wall; fine-art prints, quality posters, and most photographs carry an even lower price tag and can make accessorizing affordable.

Display

Whereas it is relatively easy to group a few small family photographs or small framed prints on a table or desk in a manner that's pleasing to the eye and complementary to the setting, displaying artwork on a wall presents more of a challenge. Whether you're considering a single painting, a collection of old maps, or a grouping of photos, the same questions arise. Where should the artwork be placed on the wall and how high off the floor? Will it fit the space visually and physically? Will it relate to the nearby furnishings and the room as a whole? Can the wall support its weight? What kind of frame is appropriate? What about lighting?

Location

Visually speaking, artwork as a whole—whether composed of a single piece or a group of items—should fit the scale and proportion of the wall it accessorizes, harmonize with furnishings (especially those that sit nearby), and be part of the total room design. As the eye flows over furnishings and follows the line of the artwork up and across the wall, it should detect a satisfying rhythm and balance.

The arrangement needn't be symmetrical as long as the size of the various elements on the wall balance each other.

Since envisioning a wall arrangement before it's actually in place may be difficult, you

can use the elevations from your furniture plan to help out. Lay a piece of tissue paper over the elevation of the wall in question and experiment with positioning the artwork in various ways. (Remember to draw it to the correct scale for the plan.) If you're intending to use a group of pictures, you can sketch in the outline of the grouping as a whole to see how the overall shape fits the wall; once that looks in balance, you can try out different configurations for the individual pictures in the collection.

Your preplanning should take into consideration the physical state of the wall itself. An interior partition may not be able to withstand the weight of a heavy painting, so you may have to relocate it to an exterior, or load-bearing, wall. Nails and hooks can pull out of the wall unless fastened to a stud (part of the structural framework) underneath. If a stud isn't located where you want to hang the picture, you can use an expansion bolt instead of a nail. The picture hooks that come with an adhesive backing are handy to use and simple to install, but they won't stick to a textured wall or support much weight.

Once you're satisfied with the approximate location of the artwork, you can begin to look for just the right frame for its display.

Framing

Though not every piece of artwork needs to be framed—posters, for instance, can often be tacked up as is—most will hang better, last longer, and look more attractive in a frame. The primary function of a

frame is a practical one—to help artwork keep its shape and to protect it against damage from handling and exposure to dust, grease, pollutants, and excess moisture or dryness in the air. But a frame also has important aesthetic functions—primarily to enhance the art itself, and secondarily to ease the transition from artwork to the surrounding background. A simple frame encourages the eye to linger on the art before taking in the rest of the wall and the overall setting. Although some artwork lends itself to a decorative or bold frame, in which the two elements work together to create a composition, the key to successful framing is not to let the frame compete with or overwhelm the art.

Occasionally, the background competes with the art, due to a patterned wallcovering or an intense paint color. One way to ease the transition and provide a buffer against the surroundings is to use a mat around the art.

Mats can also be particularly useful in enhancing small-scale artwork or delicate pastels and watercolors by setting them off with a border that becomes a visual extension of the frame.

Most of the time glass is recommended to protect the surface of the artwork from nicks and grime, but it can present some problems. Regular glass can act as a mirror and cause reflections and uncomfortable glare, which detract from the art beneath; nonreflective glass tends to dull and flatten colors. Paintings done in oil and acrylics are usually not covered with glass

Tips for Hanging and Displaying Artwork

With the framed artwork ready to be hung on the wall, it's tempting to begin hammering the fastenings. But before you make the first hole, consider the following.

• A small picture or small grouping of pictures looks better with a piece of furniture beneath it; a large or dominant piece of art can stand alone as a focal point.

• A rule of thumb for positioning artwork is to place it at eye level, but eye level differs from person to person and from place to place. A revised rule of thumb might be to hang artwork at a level that's comfortable to view from the place used most often.

• In a room with a high ceiling, positioning artwork slightly above the spot you'd normally use will draw the eye upward and pull the ceiling down; a horizontal arrangement will help counteract the height of the wall.

• In a room with a low ceiling, you can place the display somewhat lower than normal to make the ceiling seem proportionally higher; a narrow or somewhat vertical configuration of pictures will help offset the wall's horizontal lines.

• In a narrow room, a grouping that extends across the short wall will seem to widen it. If the wall is both tall and narrow, a broad configuration will help the overall proportions.

• If the individual artwork is small in size or simple in subject matter, a tight-knit grouping will create more of an impact than a widespread arrangement. Groupings typically need some common thread to link the individual items together—perhaps the same artist or theme, the same medium or color combinations.

• You can be flexible with the framing style within groupings: Use identical frames and mats and vary the sizes and shapes of the art; match the sizes of prints and frames but vary the colors of mats; use identical mats and vary the styles and depths of the frames. There are no rules, but maintaining visual balance is important.

• If you plan to display black-and-white photographs and color prints in the same arrangement, be sure that the colors don't take over—especially if the photographs are old and faded.

• Hanging artwork on the wall above the fireplace is not recommended unless the firebox has doors that can be closed to prevent damage from smoke, soot, and excessive heat.

• Keep artwork out of direct sunlight; if illuminating it with incandescent light, don't position the bulbs too close.

• Depending on the location and size of the artwork, it may be lit by uplights setting on a table or the floor, by fixtures clamped to a nearby shelf, or—most flexibly—by track lighting mounted on the ceiling. A regular incandescent flood-type bulb will light a large expanse with its wide beam; a low-voltage halogen lamp will provide a narrow, more intense and focused beam.

because the moisture in the medium can foster the growth of mildew. Prints, watercolors, pastels, and photographs framed under glass should be mounted and matted with acid-free paper or board, which won't deteriorate and cause discoloration. You can substitute lightweight, shatterproof, clear acrylic for glass in some instances, but the material produces static electricity, which attracts dust and can pull the powder of charcoals and pastels away from the surface of the art.

Hanging Artwork

Arranging artwork is something of an art in itself. If you're hanging a single painting or print, you need to be certain that it's positioned at a comfortable eye level, which may be different depending on whether it's to be seen from a sitting position most of the time, or viewed as you walk down the hall or up the stairs. Arranging a group of pictures takes even more thought, so you might like to try out the following exercise. It will give you a more accurate impression of the final effect than the elevations can.

Begin with a paper square or rectangle slightly larger than the wall area you wish to cover. Newsprint is ideal—it's inexpensive and easy to handle—or you can use an old white or light-colored sheet if you prefer. Lay the paper or sheet on the floor and arrange the artwork until you achieve the balance, shape, and visual weight that pleases you.

Trace the outline of each frame with a pencil (use chalk on the sheet). Tape the mock-up on the wall in the exact place you plan to position the grouping. Study it from close-up and afar, from sitting and standing. Leave it on the wall for a day or two to be certain that the display is where you want it. You may decide to rearrange one or two elements, changing the spacing between pictures to make the configuration tighter or more open.

While the marked-up paper or sheet hangs on the wall, keep the artwork close by, preferably on a table or the floor, and laid out in the same manner. Having the artwork near the area where it will hang allows you to examine it in the natural and artificial light it will receive and in the context of nearby furnishings.

If you change the arrangement in one place, change it in the other as well. When you are satisfied with the results, and you know the exact position of each part of the grouping, mark the precise placement of the nail, hook, or fastener on the wall mock-up. Tap the tip of a nail through the paper or sheet to mark the wall lightly. After you remove the paper, double-check the location of the various fasteners before you secure them in place.

Accenting With Plants

Even people who are not plant lovers may enjoy a container or two of natural greenery in their living spaces. Plants seem to make people feel better emotionally. They introduce color, texture, and beauty; they provide aesthetic appeal; and as decorative accessories they are highly versatile.

Plants also have a useful function in the home. They can make a sparsely furnished room look less bare—and sometimes even take the place of furnishings where there are none, perhaps on a stair landing or in the front hall. A large specimen can lend special character to a room—as a grandfather clock might do—and become a secondary focal point. Plants can serve as screens and room dividers, direct traffic flow, take the place of window coverings, and hide flaws.

Architectural Interest

Plants can also be used as architectural elements to bring unity and balance to a room. The rounded form of a large fern can contrast with and soften the rectangular or boxy lines of a table, or be used to echo the curved back of a sofa. The mass created by a branching or fountainlike plant may be used to both visually balance and repeat door or window shapes elsewhere in the room. An upright specimen can counteract too many horizontal lines. A tall, spindly plant occupying a corner next to an oversized armchair will appear underscaled, but a combination of tall, medium, and low greenery in a pyramid shape will give impor-

tance to the corner and provide the proper scale.

Plants can also be arranged to alter one's perception of a space: Placing a large-leafed variety at the entrance to a room and a similar but smaller-leafed variety against the opposite wall will make the more distant plant seem much farther away—and the room longer. (The reverse works, too.) An airy, light-colored plant with most of its lower branches removed will provide plenty of greenery without making a small room seem crowded. By contrast, an overly large room can benefit from a dense, dark tree or a freestanding cluster of

plants that commands attention from all directions and visually diminishes space.

Small Plant Accents

Tabletop displays benefit from the addition of small plants, which offer tremendous versatility as finishing touches. They lend themselves more easily than larger varieties to last-minute accessorizing. In addition, they're relatively affordable, can be chosen to fit a particular decorating style or coordinate with a color scheme, and are easily rotated with the seasons or positioned to receive more light.

When you're selecting a plant for a small table or shelf, choose a size that's comparable to a vase or bowl you'd use in the same spot. A larger surface does well with a slightly larger plant—or a grouping of small ones. Since tabletop arrangements typically display more than just one plant or other accessory, wait to select the container until you have the vignette in place. The container should be appropriate to the size and variety of plant, have decorative value, complement the other accessories, and enhance the overall arrangement.

Plants become part of the architecture in this high-ceilinged, loft living room.

91

PUTTING IT ALL TOGETHER, ROOM BY ROOM

Every room is unique on some level, an individual expression of the people who planned its spaces, developed its design, and now use it on a daily basis. At the same time, certain types of rooms share some common problems and present similar decorating challenges. A living room, for instance, typically requires seating areas that are comfortable and functional for adults and children alike. A family room must accommodate a host of activities—from boisterous parties and play to quiet reading and watching television. A dining room, home office, bedroom—even an entry and a hall—pose their own decorating challenges.

This chapter reviews typical problems, room by room, and suggests possible solutions that may help you put together your own room project. In addition, the gallery of photographs that accompanies each grouping of rooms demonstrates how a variety of designers and homeowners met similar challenges. Seeing their solutions may offer some further points of inspiration for decorating your home.

When planning a gathering place for the family—even in a small area such as this one—be sure to include appropriate seating for all ages, durable fabrics, and adequate storage.

THE ENTRY AND HALLWAYS

However grand or modest in size, the entry, or foyer, plays a significant role in establishing a first impression of you and your home. Unlike the entry, the other passageways within the home are often overlooked in a decorating plan.

When the entry visually opens to the living room or another major living space, as often happens, it can set the stage for your decorating scheme. All too often, though, the typical entry is small, boxy, low on natural light, and none too welcoming.

You can help the area make a good impression, however, with a few decorating tricks.

Small entries take well to understated solutions. Mirrors can make the space look double its size, especially when they bounce natural light into all corners. Light colors, textured surfaces, subtle patterns, and flooring that flows into neighboring rooms further increase the feeling of spaciousness. You can furnish the entry with a grouping of small-scale furnishings to make the overall area appear larger—an occasional table just big enough to hold the mail, keys, and a petite vase of flowers, plus a small chair or bench. Or you can give the small space a greater presence with one or two larger pieces—an inviting wing chair, a handsome grandfather clock, or an antique cupboard.

If the foyer in your home is so amply sized that it seems impersonal, you can alter its nature by giving it another function. Ushering visitors into a reception area that looks and feels like a warm den or sitting room can make them feel right at home, and you can use the space for spillover dining and seating when entertaining.

The back hall, interior hallways, stairwells, and landings are sometimes regarded only as necessary connectors between living spaces—and are typically narrow and poorly lit. Hallways invariably lack space to put things down, much less store them away.

Dim halls and stairwells can be illuminated with a track lighting system that pools light on the floor to create a safer passage and washes the walls with light to visually expand the narrow dimensions. You might line the newly lit walls with old family photographs or fine-art prints for a gallery effect that's sure to elevate the space to the status of a room. Landings and the ells of halls can serve as minilibraries with the addition of floor-to-ceiling bookshelves pushed against one wall. (You can put a wide hall to work as a library, too, balancing the visual weight of books on one wall with strong color, patterned wallcoverings, or a tapestry on the other wall.)

Color and texture can do a lot to widen a narrow hall—or shorten a long one. Remembering that dark and intense colors advance, bringing surfaces visually closer, and that lighter more subdued hues recede, for the opposite effect, can be a valuable aid in planning the scheme for your halls. The back hall can become an entryway in its own right with a little attention—a practical area with hooks to hang jackets, hinge-top benches to store boots or gardening gear, attractive lockers to stash hockey sticks, softball bats, and skateboards.

Choose an appropriate flooring material for these areas of your home. Back halls are a good spot for heavy-duty, easy-clean resilients that stand up to dirt and pets. Interior halls do well with low-pile, tight-weave, commercial-style carpet that's soft underfoot but extremely durable.

Stairway walls are perfect galleries for photographs or any favorite artwork.

If your home lacks a formal entry, you can create one with a simple arrangement of small-scale furnishings and well-chosen accessories.

THE LIVING ROOM

Most living rooms occupy a unique place in the home. Typically the first room that's seen after entering the front hall, the living room is called upon to set the mood and look of the interior.

Traditionally viewed as the showpiece space in which to receive visitors, and often decorated more formally than other parts of the home, the living room in today's home is still intended to serve as an inviting and comfortable area for conversing with guests and entertaining. At the same time, it's expected to function as a flexible sitting and gathering space for family members of varying ages, builds, and interests. What sometimes happens, though, is that these diverse demands result in a living room that may look good but is neither flexible nor friendly—and, as such, becomes a mostly wasted room, an occasional living space.

To help your living room fulfill its functions and remain comfortable to family and guests, begin by deciding on a focal point around which to create conversation and sitting areas. A living room is often designed to make a stronger architectural statement than other rooms, so you might emphasize an architectural detail—a marble fireplace or a window with a striking view, for instance. Or your focus might be on a handsome wall system that incorporates the stereo and TV, a minilibrary, and a favorite collection.

By providing a variety of seating that can be moved to suit the particular need of the moment, you can entertain large or small numbers with relative ease. Love seats, wide, armless chairs, and ottomans are ideal choices for movable seating that can accommodate more than one person at a time. Intermixing low, lounge-type furnishings with upright chairs and standard-height tables within the same conversation area can also accommodate people of varying age and size. Keep in mind, too, the importance of arranging furnishings to enhance the entrance into the living space and positioning them to encourage easy circulation between the different areas of the room.

Flexible furnishings will help you plan for secondary activities you might not have considered for the living room—dining informally in front of the fireplace, setting up an impromptu game table when friends drop by, converting an out-of-the-way corner into a children's play space or reading nook. You can keep the look formal with wallcoverings and window treatments and still let children enjoy the room by using fabrics and floor coverings that are easy to maintain. Attention to lighting will also help your room be adaptable to changing functions: Table and floor lamps normally used for reading and tasks can be equipped with dimmers to create atmosphere for entertaining, and uplights placed on the floor can create dramatic ceiling and wall effects.

Although this elegant room has some formal elements, its casual seating arrangement and painted paneled walls set a relaxed tone.

Soft curves and a pastel color scheme are the main design elements in this contemporary living room. The effect is serene and elegant.

Red makes a strong visual statement in this eclectic living room. Liberal use of a single color also ties the room together.

THE DINING ROOM

Thoughts of the dining room invariably bring forth images of comfort, hospitality, good food, and relaxing times, whether the dining takes place in a room of its own, in a corner of the living room, or in an ell off the kitchen.

The space typically set aside for dining poses a logistical dilemma in many homes. It's often too small and cramped for real comfort—nicely cozy perhaps for an occasional evening meal or a Sunday dinner, but quite inadequate when it comes to seating the entire family on Thanksgiving or having a large cocktail party.

One solution for small to midsized dining areas is a small table that can be expanded for a special occasion with two or three leaves. You might also enlarge it with a false top made of particleboard or plywood; with a cloth hiding the surface, your guests will never know the difference, and the top can

be stored when not in use. On the other hand, you might prefer a nonexpandable table, and create additional dining and serving space with a drop-leaf table that's normally tucked against the wall but can be put to work as a buffet or brought farther into the room and extended to handle a large group of diners. If space is really tight, consider a shallow, wall-hung sideboard for storing china or linens; the open area underneath makes it easy to pull up chairs or stools to dine counter style. Or introduce a shallow corner cupboard or two to take advantage of normally wasted space.

Since too many chairs in a dining space of any size can seem all legs when not in use, you can place the extras in another room. As long as they are of a comfortable height and pull up to the table with relative ease, you can mix and match styles. Coordinating colors and patterns will give them a more unified appearance.

If you're lucky enough to have a large dining room, consider giving the space another job to extend its usefulness beyond a few meals a week. Many dining rooms already double as a place for children to do homework and parents to finish work they may bring home from the office. Why not go a step further and create an all-new atmosphere that enhances the dining experience while catering to other needs in the off-hours of the room—a library, perhaps, or a study-sitting room? Book and display shelves can dress up the walls while serving as buffet and storage space; a small sofa or built-in alcove can offer extra seats for dining and possibly convert to guest sleeping quarters in a pinch.

Left: Shaker-inspired ladder-back chairs serve both a formal dining table and a casual eating counter. The low-back chairs can be pulled to the table to seat extra guests. Opposite: To visually expand this small room, the dining table was placed at an angle. The corner hutch provides needed storage space and a spot to display colorful tableware.

THE FAMILY ROOM

Topping the list as a favorite spot to put up your feet and let down your hair is the family room. It's the place where all kinds of functions rub shoulders and sometimes go on at the same time: listening to music and practicing it or playing quiet board games and wrestling on the floor.

The easy-going activities of the family room can leave the room in disarray, unless materials are chosen to suit the family life-style, and spaces are organized to accommodate the various activities that take place. In many instances, the family room is the only area of the home where watching TV or a movie on the VCR accompanies after-school snacks or after-dinner coffee, where electronic games and jigsaw puzzles, parents' books, and children's toys all share the same territory. Furthermore, if the children are young, and pets live in the household, there's bound to be romping around, additional noise, and extra maintenance.

Offsetting an unkempt appearance, and encouraging youngsters to pick up and put things away, can be accomplished by having lots of convenient storage within easy reach: trunks and blanket chests as coffee tables and storage bins; old hatboxes and wooden crates to hold small toys; wall units with closed storage on the bottom for children's possessions, open shelving above for magazines and books to please the older crowd. Depending on your personal tastes, you can either allow the TV and video equipment to remain out in the open or keep them mostly out of sight behind closed doors.

Maintenance and noise can both be reduced with a careful choice of coverings for walls, floors, and furnishings. Patterned carpets with a low, dense pile hide dirt and stains as admirably as they muffle noise and offer soft sitting surfaces; wood paneling and heavy, vinyl-coated wallcoverings wipe clean as readily as they absorb sound. Practical, durable furnishings are a must in family room settings, with upholstered seating covered with soil-retardant fabrics or washable slipcovers, wood tables and cabinetry protected with impervious finishes.

In even a small family room, space can be found for a separate play area for the young set. You can screen off a portion of the room with a low divider, furnishings, a folding partition, or a grouping of plants. By equipping the area with a low table and chairs and places for storage, you can provide your children and their friends some freedom to express themselves without intruding on the rest of the family.

Accessible storage, such as these inexpensive plastic crates, makes it easy for children to clean up after playtime. Modular shelving keeps the television in view but out of the way.

Top: The details that make this small attic family room such an appealing space will transfer successfully to any size room: bright colors, multiuse storage, and activity areas for games, reading, and relaxing. Bottom: Attractive modular units provide all-purpose storage for books, games, a television, and other electronic equipment.

THE BEDROOM

It frequently happens that bedrooms are the last rooms to receive attention in home decorating plans, all too often making do as rather plain areas for sleeping and grooming. But they can offer far more than quiet and comfort alone.

Bedrooms are too often characterized by a bed that dominates the space, a nightstand and dresser, and a closet that's never big enough. With inadequate storage, books can stack up in piles, toys spill on the floor, clothes bulge out of drawers—and the room becomes less than a welcome retreat. Even the master suite, typically larger than the other bedrooms and better equipped with closet space, presents challenges in figuring out how to organize areas for sleeping, dressing, sitting, working—or working out.

Built-in storage can be a small bedroom's best friend, and offers a fine solution to organizing the overall area, helping to define zones, and making even a king-sized bed seem to take up far less space. Built-ins come in several forms. You can purchase modular furnishings that fit together in a variety of ways to provide flexible storage systems that can be disassembled and reconfigured as needs change. Or you can order a customized built-in system (or have one built on site by a carpenter) designed and fabricated to fit your spaces precisely and take advantage of literally every corner, angle, nook, and cranny.

If your budget can't accommodate the cost of custom built-ins, you can still create the feeling of them with standard furnishings and a little

Crisp linens, soft fabrics, wall-to-wall carpeting, and a warm color scheme make this master bedroom a pleasing retreat.

imagination. Pull the bed into the center of the room and fit a bookcase against one end to act as headboard plus divider between the sleeping zone and a book-lined sitting space, study, homework station, or exercise area. Buy an unfinished armoire or a secondhand wardrobe and custom-plan the interior to hold a TV, stereo equipment, and so forth in one section, clothing or bedding in another. Create a window seat niche without a real niche by lining the under-window wall

with side-by-side blanket chests, matching wicker trunks, or a row of storage cubes, then topping them all with comfortable cushions that coordinate with window dressings.

Storage concerns aside, creating a comfortable and restful atmosphere in the bedroom takes high priority—especially in the master bedroom. Fabrics on walls and windows, soft floor coverings, and plump upholstered furnishings can underscore a quiet mood, muffling noise from other rooms

and the street. If you own a beautiful bed—a carved wood four-poster or a brass antique—you might wish to let it stand out as the focal point of the room and play down the background. (On the other hand, if your bed is simply average in appearance, you can play up the windows and walls with color and pattern and put emphasis on another piece of furniture, such as a lovely old desk or a new wing chair and ottoman.)

Children's bedrooms, too, require quiet and comfort and storage, but they also need to be fun, flexibly furnished, and easy to grow up with. Involving your children in the design of their rooms and incorporating their ideas alongside yours will help the space function at its best and perhaps stay relatively tidy. You can assist even toddlers in keeping their rooms neat by providing many storage alternatives: colorful rubber dishpans and wire baskets for small toys; low-to-the-floor shelving for bulkier items and puzzles; rows of easy-reach hooks to hang up clothes. Durable furnishings with easy-clean surfaces are a must for almost any age youngster—not to mention flooring that can stand up to abuse.

When children share the bedroom with a sibling or invite friends to stay overnight on a frequent basis, the sleeping arrangements can take several turns: space-saving bunk beds keep the floor area open and are ideal for a very small room; platform beds typically have a series of built-in drawers and storage compartments underneath the bed, eliminating the need for bulky, freestanding bureaus; trundle beds pull out from under a standard-height bed like a giant sleeping drawer—and push back in just as easily; Murphy beds pull down and out of the wall from behind closed doors and fold back up when not in use.

Easy-care materials and furnishings are a must for a child's bedroom. If there is an extra bed so that a friend can spend the night, all the better.

DUAL-PURPOSE ROOMS

Today's homes seldom have enough space to let a spare room sit idle. More likely, the now–extra bedroom is put to use as a combination den-guest room, or a sewing space, study, and office all rolled into one.

In any dual- or triple-purpose room, decide first on the primary function of the area, then tailor its other jobs to fit the setting and still stand on their own. If, for instance, a study takes precedence over guest quarters in the same space, and privacy and lack of noise are the major concerns, you might cover the walls with fabric rather than paper or paint, insulate a potentially noisy wall (one with a hallway or family room on the other side, for instance) with book-lined shelves, carpet the floor, or bring in a comfortable sofa or daybed to serve as a relaxing reading spot when you're not at the desk. When the study turns into a guest room, the sofa can convert to a bed, and a side table with drawers or a chest can become a mini-dresser. If you set up a portable TV and a coffee maker on the desk or the bookshelves, your guest will feel even more welcome.

Whether your need for a home office is simply a place to pay bills and file paperwork, or one that must function as a business office five days a

week, the key to success lies in the planning. Excellent permanent storage to hold clutter and facilitate keeping track of things, well-defined work surfaces, and proper lighting are all necessary for the efficient home office, large or small.

If a minioffice is all you need, clever planning may help you squeeze a work space into an out-of-the way spot: under the stairs, into a little-used closet, in an ell of a hall or a corner of the laundry room. For appearance' sake, it helps to close off even a small office from view. If you like to spread things out or require a large work surface and open-shelf storage, arrange for a way to shut off the area visually—with a folding screen, bifold or pocket doors, a freestanding partition, even a matchstick or fabric shade to lower from the ceiling.

The serious home office that demands more than a small personal computer can be a challenge to incorporate into tight quarters. It typically requires more physical space to meet the requirements of a regular office, including file cabi-

nets and substantial shelving, and often must accommodate a fair amount of electronic equipment—from a keyboard and printer to a photocopier and fax machine. An office of this nature can also be more difficult to treat as a dual-purpose room. An office-cum-guest room, for instance, can disrupt your work schedule and your guest's privacy and comfort unless the essentials of your trade can be easily relocated to a temporary post. On the other hand, sharing an office with a sewing or an exercise area, a small studio, or a study might function smoothly if the various activities are flexibly scheduled. Again, careful planning is the secret to putting it all together.

Left: An efficient office doesn't need much square footage to function successfully. This "computer closet" makes clever use of an otherwise-ignored space.
Opposite: Even if the formal dining room is your family's daily eating area, it can also serve another function. Inexpensive storage cubes show off collectibles on upper shelves, and lower cubes house a personal library. Between meals the dining table can function as a desk for homework or as a work surface for any project in progress.

THE KITCHEN AND BATH

Improving the kitchen and bath to function at their best generally falls into the realm of remodeling, a subject that this book doesn't address. But there are several cosmetic improvements you can implement in the kitchen and bathroom with minimal expense and disruption to your daily life.

Often just perking up these areas of your home can make them—and you—feel like new. Making a kitchen lighter and brighter can help it seem larger and more functional. If you're tired of the look of the cabinets, consider covering the door fronts with a heavy-duty, vinyl-coated wallcovering that matches or coordinates with one on the walls. A slightly textured surface offers visual interest, yet is easy to keep clean. Painting the rest of the cabinetry and the ceiling a color that's close in tint or shade will provide continuity and make the room appear larger. If the upper cabinets seem to close in on the space, remove the doors altogether in one section to put colorful pottery, mugs, or china on display; a fresh coat of paint on all cabinet surfaces will tie together both open and closed shelving. Dark-stained cabinets can make a kitchen gloomy, so you might look into hiring a refinisher to bleach the wood. The pleasure derived may well outweigh the cost.

Finding enough storage and counter space is nearly always an issue in the kitchen. A compact island on wheels can help ease the pressure, providing a work surface on top and self-contained storage beneath.

If a quick visual fix is all you have in mind, simply redecorate the background and introduce new accessories. Create faux paint finishes on walls, ceiling, and floor; choose a completely different window treatment; cover chair and stool cushions with a cheerful, easy-care fabric; change the knobs and drawer pulls in cabinet fronts for hardware with a more updated look; buy new pots for your old plants and a canister set to match your new color scheme.

If kitchen walls, cabinets, and floors are kept neutral, a change of accessories will transform the space. Here, soft Austrian shades and matching seat cushions provide the decorative accents, as does the floral needlepoint rug.

Like kitchens, bathrooms can get a fresh outlook from a simple face-lift. You may not be able to change unappealing, outdated tile, but a clever paint scheme or a well-chosen wallcovering can make it less noticeable. Lackluster tile can be sparked with a new decorative tile border that echoes the wallcovering design or the colors of the flooring material. Mirrors are an excellent way to increase the apparent size of a small bath. Position them so that sunlight doesn't hit the surface directly, however, or create uncomfortable glare. Mirrors, too, are essential to the rituals of grooming, as is the presence of even, flattering light. Ideally, mirrors are illuminated with a series of small lamps around the perimeter; if that's not possible, install a row on each side. (Artificial light from above tends to cast shadows that interfere with shaving and putting on makeup.) If the bathroom lighting comes from a fixture in the center of the room, consider installing a small track system to shine light into corners and wash walls for more even general lighting. In any event, convert to dimmer switches so that you can control the amount and intensity of the light.

You can disguise a homely shower-tub with new frosted and etched doors, or less expensively with an attractive fabric curtain hung over a waterproof liner. If you have a little leeway in your budget, consider a new finish on the porcelain tub and sink—there are companies who specialize in resurfacing fixtures—or call in a carpenter to adapt the antique cabinet you recently acquired to house the existing sink.

Most bathrooms have limited storage and not enough space to hang damp towels. When several family members use the same bath, additional towel racks can be installed in a staggered pattern at different heights. Foldaway wood or metal clothes dryers are another practical solution. Or you can outfit the back of the door with dowels or a rack that pulls away from the door when needed and lies flush when not in use. You can create extra space to stash linens, grooming supplies, and so forth in out-of-the way places: Storage cubes or rectangular baskets can be turned on their side for easy access to items and stacked in one or more corners; shelves that extend to the ceiling can be added over the toilet—and even over the window and door.

Clever use of wallpaper, borders, and moldings adds charm and elegance to a small guest bath. Painting the upper walls a dark color made the tall ceiling appear lower.

Black and white marble tiles cover the floor and part of one wall in this lively bathroom. The same effect can be achieved with resilient tile. Mirrors above the sink and on one wall open up the room.

POSITIONING THE TV

From the time that television first became popular in American homes some forty-odd years ago, it has presented a perpetual challenge: how to assimilate it into living spaces without letting it dominate them.

Initially, the television was usually kept in the living room of most homes, often as a freestanding console that resembled a piece of furniture. As it became less bulky, and then portable, the television could be found in many more rooms. Now, it's a fixture in nearly every family room and is frequently found in the workshop, the kitchen, the children's bedrooms, and the master bedroom suite.

The question remains, however, whether this ubiquitous fixture should be left out in the open, given a low profile, or disguised altogether. And the answer is purely personal. Electronics enthusiasts might want the area of the family room that houses the TV, stereo, and VCR to feel like a media room, with an entertainment center that displays the equipment with a combination of open shelves and glass-front cabinets. Large, high-quality screens and slim lines make some televisions ideal candidates for placement in a narrow wall system that doesn't intrude in a small room; shallow shelves and storage around the big screen can help downplay its size.

If you want to de-emphasize the TV when it's not in use, you can hide the unit inside an armoire or a large cupboard, or even in a specially outfitted closet. Just be certain that interior shelving can accommodate the television, its wiring, and any related equipment or gadgetry, and that the set itself be on a swivel shelf or turntable that can be pulled away from the cabinet to allow easy viewing from more than one spot. As an alternative, you might consider a custom cabinet or a built-in arrangement that is designed and fabricated to fit a particular space in your room—an option that may not necessarily be more costly than buying ready-made furnishings and perhaps be more in keeping with your decorating style.

Wherever you put the TV, avoid causing glare on the screen from reflected daylight or artificial lighting. Angling the screen to benefit one viewer may make it worse for another seated elsewhere in the room. Ideally, the set should be positioned to avoid reflections; if they can't be avoided, install window coverings such as shades, blinds, or simple drapes, which can be drawn or pulled down to adjust the amount of light.

A freestanding cabinet provides attractive storage for a television. This cabinet has the simple, straightforward lines of American country, but similar units are available to suit almost any decorating style.

With the addition of built-in closets and a window-height media center, plus plump, upholstered furniture, a spare bedroom becomes a cozy, appealing family room/guest room.

SOLVING PROBLEM STORAGE

Figuring out where to stow things, especially odd-shaped and bulky items, is a challenge in every part of the house.

When the back hall doesn't have the space for anything beyond a small storage cabinet, you might look to the laundry or utility room. By organizing shelving and closet space in an orderly fashion and replacing freestanding items, such as the worktable and ironing board, with foldaway versions, you can create extra room to store some of the things that don't fit anyplace else: sports equipment, the vacuum cleaner, recycling bins, large bags of dog food, and gardening tools.

The garage may offer additional storage possibilities. Even if the cars take up every inch of floor area, you can utilize the space above them. Suspend bicycles, canoes, and sleds from sturdy hooks; store helmets, oars, and volleyballs and nets—anything that's not too small or heavy—in net bags or a hammock that also hang from hooks. Stash skis, rakes, and shovels in the narrow vertical space between studs, and tuck in some narrow shelves here and there to hold small objects. You can also span the rafters with plywood to make a loft for storing luggage, or boxes of out-of-season clothes.

Open wire-mesh baskets—one for each family member—ease laundry sorting and toting.

INDEX

U.S./Metric Measure Conversion Chart

	Symbol	When you know:	Multiply by:	To find:	Rounded Measures for Quick Reference		
		Formulas for Exact Measures					
Mass (Weight)	oz	ounces	28.35	grams	1 oz		= 30 g
	lb	pounds	0.45	kilograms	4 oz		= 115 g
	g	grams	0.035	ounces	8 oz		= 225 g
	kg	kilograms	2.2	pounds	16 oz	= 1 lb	= 450 g
					32 oz	= 2 lb	= 900 g
					36 oz	= 2¼ lb	= 1000 g (1 kg)
Volume	tsp	teaspoons	5.0	milliliters	¼ tsp	= ⅛ oz	= 1 ml
	tbsp	tablespoons	15.0	milliliters	½ tsp	= 1/12 oz	= 2 ml
	fl oz	fluid ounces	29.57	milliliters	1 tsp	= ⅙ oz	= 5 ml
	c	cups	0.24	liters	1 tbsp	= ½ oz	= 15 ml
	pt	pints	0.47	liters	1 c	= 8 oz	= 250 ml
	qt	quarts	0.95	liters	2 c (1 pt)	= 16 oz	= 500 ml
	gal	gallons	3.785	liters	4 c (1 qt)	= 32 oz	= 1 liter
	ml	milliliters	0.034	fluid ounces	4 qt (1 gal)	= 128 oz	= 3¾ liter
Length	in.	inches	2.54	centimeters	⅜ in.	= 1 cm	
	ft	feet	30.48	centimeters	1 in.	= 2.5 cm	
	yd	yards	0.9144	meters	2 in.	= 5 cm	
	mi	miles	1.609	kilometers	2½ in.	= 6.5 cm	
	km	kilometers	0.621	miles	12 in. (1 ft)	= 30 cm	
	m	meters	1.094	yards	1 yd	= 90 cm	
	cm	centimeters	0.39	inches	100 ft	= 30 m	
					1 mi	= 1.6 km	
Temperature	° F	Fahrenheit	5/9 (after subtracting 32)	Celsius	32° F	= 0° C	
	° C	Celsius	9/5 (then add 32)	Fahrenheit	68° F	= 20° C	
					212° F	= 100° C	
Area	in.²	square inches	6.452	square centimeters	1 in.²	= 6.5 cm²	
	ft²	square feet	929.0	square centimeters	1 ft²	= 930 cm²	
	yd²	square yards	8361.0	square centimeters	1 yd²	= 8360 cm²	
	a.	acres	0.4047	hectares	1 a.	= 4050 m²	